Quick Guitar Chords

Simple
Search

No-Fuss,
Flick-thru
Guides

Jake Jackson

Publisher and Creative Director: Nick Wells

Project, design and media integration: Jake Jackson

Website and software: David Neville with Stevens Dumpala and Steve Moulton

Editorial: Gillian Whitaker

First published 2022 by
FLAME TREE PUBLISHING
6 Melbray Mews
Fulham, London SW6 3NS
United Kingdom
flametreepublishing.com

Music information site:
flametreemusic.com

26 25 24 23 22
10 9 8 7 6 5 4 3 2 1

ISBN: 978-1-83964-890-8

Printed and bound in the UK by Clays Ltd, Elcograf S.p.A.

The CIP record for this book is available from the British Library.

Jake Jackson is a writer and musician. He has created and contributed to over 20 practical music books, including *Reading Music Made Easy*, *Play Flamenco* and *Piano and Keyboard Chords*. His music is available on iTunes, Amazon and Spotify amongst others.

See & Hear
Web Links

Acoustic &
Electric

Quick Guitar Chords

Simple
Search

No-Fuss,
Flick-thru
Guides

Jake Jackson

Flame Tree
Music
CHORDS • SCALES
flametreemusic.com

Contents

Online access
flametreemusic.com
Scan the code
to hear the chord

4

The Chords

Online access
flametreemusic.com

Scan the code
to hear the chord

Introduction

Chords are the building blocks for every budding musician. Stringing together a few triads can liberate a melody and, being easy to communicate, will help you play with others. QUICK GUITAR CHORDS combines a solid approach to chord diagrams with an integrated, online sound solution.

When I first started to play the guitar I bought a cheap steel-string acoustic, an Epiphone. I saw it in the window of a guitar shop I passed every day. It was surrounded by more glamorous instruments, mainly electic-blue Fender Strats and sunburst Gibson Les Pauls. But, at the price, I loved the look of it – the full body, the slim neck – and eventually saved up enough money to buy it, steeling myself for the inevitable complaints from my neighbours.

It didn't go well at first. In later years I came to realize that the cheaper the guitar, the harder it is to play, but at the time the strings were so far off the neck I could barely press them down and I suffered weeks of physical agony, nearly giving up. But I had a friend and he had a heavy wooden guitar, a beast, a Westone Thunder. I watched his impossibly big fingers float across the frets as he made the music dance, so he kept me inspired. And he was patient; oh, boy was he patient.

Eventually I could press down the strings, and continued with some simple chords, E minor, A minor, I think, and a top-three-string G major and a D major. Well, it's incredible how many

songs can come from just these four chords! Of course I tried loads of chord books. A decent one is not ashamed of its reader because simplicity is essential at any level. You want to see the chord, understand it quickly and play it (I still do).

Of course the more you play, the more curious you get. And, when you're looking for new sounds, a new feel always comes from a new chord: it's very useful to explore the 6ths and the 9ths, and when your fingers are warm and loose, try some of the 7sus4s and 11ths, or 13ths. In the early days, I used to have a songwriting rule: every new tune would contain something new, for me, sometimes it was a rhythm, sometimes a new verse-chorus structure, but most often, it was a new chord. Using a new set of notes can spring life into a tired bag of basic chords and force your developing musical brain into new territory.

So, chords are important to every songwriter, but especially for anyone playing with others, arranging and working out chord progressions. This new book offers just the first position on 20 chords per key. It gives you a great range to experiment with and, combined with the power of mobile technology, you can hear how the chord is meant to sound by using a smartphone camera and any free QR reader app. Connected to the flametreemusic.com website you can hear each chord on the piano and the guitar, and a second guitar position too.

This is such a great tool, a unique experience that will give you hours of productive fun, whether you're bashing out some great songs, or playing with others. Good Luck!

Jake Jackson

Online access
flametreemusic.com

Scan the code
to hear the chord

The Chord Diagrams

The diagrams in this book are for chord shapes. There are twenty chords for each key. Each chord is shown in the first position, near the nut.

By understanding the notes on the neck you can work out the second and third positions using the same notes further up the neck. You can also create inversions of a chord by changing the order of notes.

Standard Notation

When playing with others it is also helpful to understand the basis of music notation by matching the notes below to the finger positions on the guitar (*see* page 11). This will help you identify chords and see how melodies can be constructed.

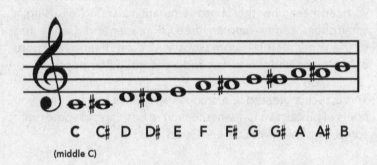

C C♯ D D♯ E F F♯ G G♯ A A♯ B

(middle C)

Online access
flametreemusic.com   Scan the code
to hear the chord

8

GUITAR CHORDS

The Strings: The bass E appears on the left (6th string).
The top E is on the right (1st string).
The top E is the E above **middle C** on the piano.

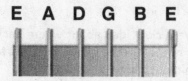

E A D G B E

Fingerings: ① is the index finger ② is the middle finger
③ is the ring finger ④ is the little finger

String isn't played

Open string position

Nut at the top of the neck

The 1st fret

Finger position for the notes

This is a barre chord: the finger stretches across the fret, pressing on more than one string

3

When the chord position isn't close to the nut, the number indicates the fret position.

Notes in the chord

Chord Spelling
1st (A), 3rd (C♯), 5th (E), ♭7th (G), 9th (B)

Notes on the Neck

It's useful to have a clear idea about where each note lies in relation to other notes. On the guitar, the frets are organized in half-note (semitone) intervals.

Chord Construction

Chords are based on three-note triads with a root note being the lowest note, and usually the indicator of the chord. With six strings the guitar allows you to repeat notes an octave higher or lower to create a rich sound.

Because the guitar has a three- to four-octave range, and some notes can be played at exactly the same pitch in several fingerboard positions, the harmonic possibilities on the instrument are almost endless: even simple major or minor chords can be played in numerous fingerboard positions – each with a multitude of possible fingerings.

Chord Shapes

Use shapes that suit your fingers and which work quickly with the other chord shapes you're playing in a song. Often you'll find that, rather than having to stretch around the fingerboard to play the next chord, you can devise an alternative fingering near to the previous chord.

Online access
flametreemusic.com

Scan the code
to hear the chord

The notes at the top of the diagram (**E A D G B E**) are the open strings, played without fingers pressing down.

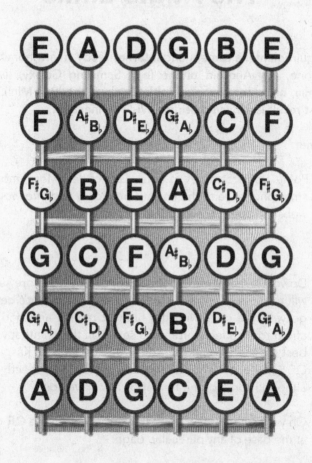

The bass **E** is on the left, the **6th string**. The **1st string**, on the right, is also **E**, but **two octaves above** the bass **E**, the 6th string.

The Audio Links

Requirements: a camera and internet-ready smartphone (e.g. iPhone, any Android phone (e.g. Samsung Galaxy), Nokia Lumia, or camera-enabled tablet such as the iPad Mini). The best result is achieved using a Wi-Fi connection.

Either:

1. Point your camera at the QR code. Most modern smartphones read the link automatically and offer you the website **flametreemusic.com** to connect online.

Or:

1. Download any **free QR code reader**. An app store search will reveal a great many of these, so obviously it's best to go with the ones with the highest ratings and don't be afraid to try a few before you settle on the one that works best for you. Tapmedia's QR Code Reader app, Kaspersky QR Scanner or QR Code Reader by Scan are perfectly fine, although some of the free apps also have ads.

2. On your smartphone, open the app and **scan** the **QR code** at the base of any particular page.

Online access
flametreemusic.com

Scan the code
to hear the chord

Then:

3. Scanning the chord will bring you to the chord page. From there you can access and **hear** the complete library of scales and chords on **flametreemusic.com**.

   On pages where QR codes feature alongside particular chords and scales, those codes will take you directly to the relevant chord or scale on the website.

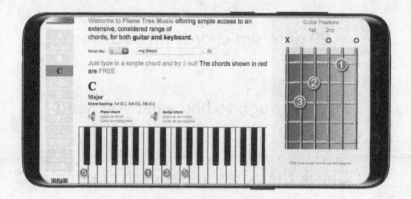

4. Use the drop-down menu to choose from **20 scales** or 12 **free chords** (50 with subscription) per key.

5. Click the sounds! Both piano and guitar audio is provided. This is particularly helpful when you're playing with others.

   The QR codes give you direct access to chords and scales. You can access a much wider range of chords if you register.

Online access
flametreemusic.com

Scan the code
to hear the chord

Easy Access

Organized from A to G keys

•

20 different chords for each key

•

Flick through to find what you need

•

Check the notes under each diagram

•

Use the QR code to hear the chord

•

Online access
flametreemusic.com

Scan the code
to hear the chord

Quick Guitar Chords

Simple Search

No-Fuss, Flick-thru Guides

A
Major

Chord Spelling
1st (A), 3rd (C#), 5th (E)

Am
Minor

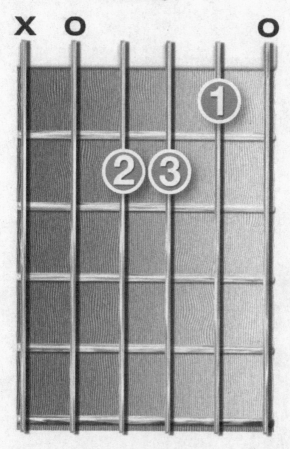

Chord Spelling
1st (A), ♭3rd (C), 5th (E)

A+
Augmented Triad

X   X

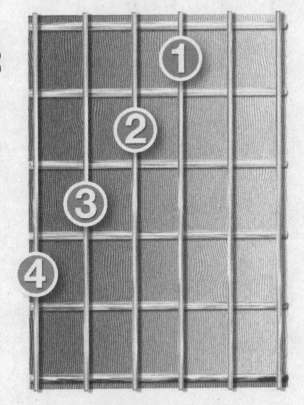

Chord Spelling

1st (A), 3rd (C#), #5th (E#)

Online access
flametreemusic.com

Scan the code
to hear the chord

A°
Diminished Triad

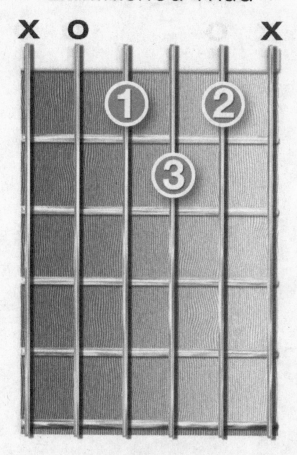

Chord Spelling
1st (A), ♭3rd (C), ♭5th (E♭)

Asus2
Suspended 2nd

Chord Spelling
1st (A), 2nd (B), 5th (E)

Online access
flametreemusic.com

Scan the code
to hear the chord

Asus4
Suspended 4th

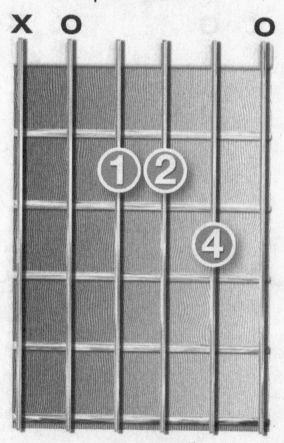

Chord Spelling
1st (A), 4th (D), 5th (E)

Online access
flametreemusic.com Scan the code
to hear the chord

A5

5th (Power Chord)

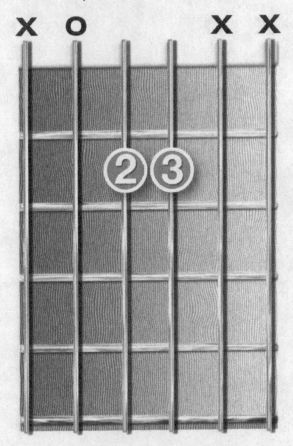

Chord Spelling

1st (A), 5th (E)

Online access
flametreemusic.com

Scan the code
to hear the chord

A6
Major 6th

Chord Spelling

1st (A), 3rd (C#), 5th (E), 6th (F#)

Online access
flametreemusic.com Scan the code
to hear the chord

Am6
Minor 6th

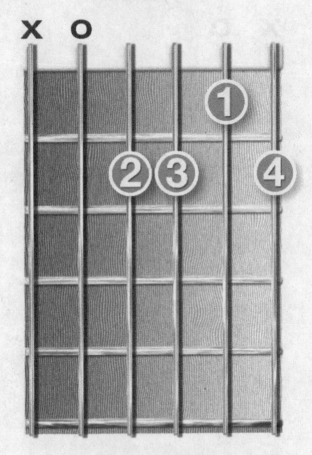

Chord Spelling
1st (A), ♭3rd (C), 5th (E), 6th (F♯)

Online access
flametreemusic.com

Scan the code
to hear the chord

A6sus4
6th Suspended 4th

Chord Spelling

1st (A), 4th (D), 5th (E), 6th (F#)

Online access
flametreemusic.com Scan the code
to hear the chord

Amaj7
Major 7th

Chord Spelling

1st (A), 3rd (C#), 5th (E), 7th (G#)

Am7
Minor 7th

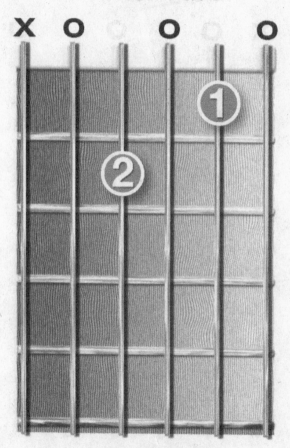

Chord Spelling
1st (A), ♭3rd (C), 5th (E), ♭7th (G)

Online access
flametreemusic.com Scan the code
to hear the chord

A7
Dominant 7th

Chord Spelling

1st (A), 3rd (C#), 5th (E), ♭7th (G)

A°7
Diminished 7th

Chord Spelling
1st (A), ♭3rd (C), ♭5th (E♭), ♭♭7th (G♭)

A7sus4

Dominant 7th Suspended 4th

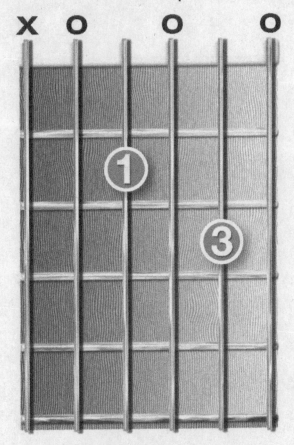

Chord Spelling

1st (A), 4th (D), 5th (E), ♭7th (G)

Online access
flametreemusic.com

Scan the code
to hear the chord

Amaj9
Major 9th

Chord Spelling

1st (A), 3rd (C#), 5th (E), 7th (G#), 9th (B)

Online access
flametreemusic.com

Scan the code
to hear the chord

Am9
Minor 9th

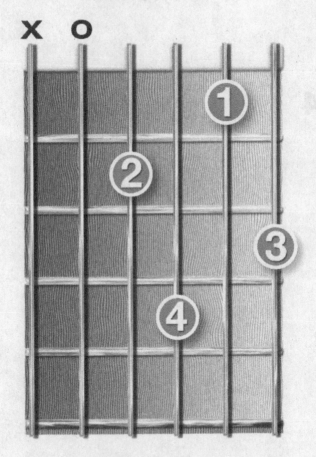

Chord Spelling
1st (A), ♭3rd (C), 5th (E), ♭7th (G), 9th (B)

A9
Dominant 9th

Chord Spelling
1st (A), 3rd (C♯), 5th (E), ♭7th (G), 9th (B)

Online access
flametreemusic.com

Scan the code
to hear the chord

Amaj11
Major 11th

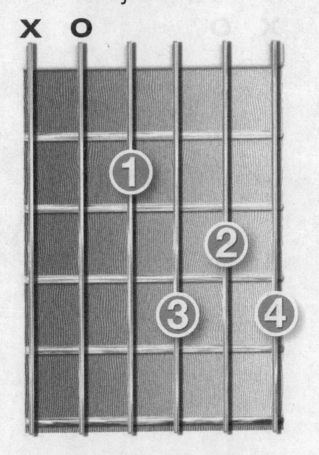

Chord Spelling

1st (A), 3rd (C#), 5th (E), 7th (G#), 9th (B), 11th (D)

Online access
flametreemusic.com

Scan the code
to hear the chord

Amaj13
Major 13th

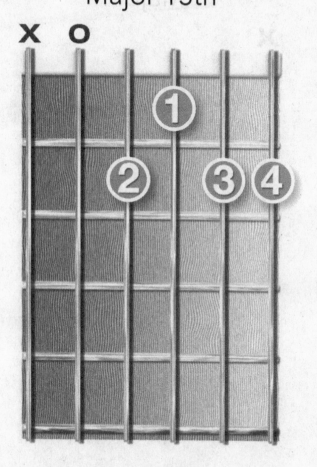

Chord Spelling

1st (A), 3rd (C#), 5th (E), 7th (G#), 9th (B), 11th (D), 13th (F#)

A#/Bb
Major

Chord Spelling
1st (Bb), 3rd (D), 5th (F)

Online access
flametreemusic.com

Scan the code
to hear the chord

A♯/B♭m
Minor

Chord Spelling
1st (B♭), ♭3rd (D♭), 5th (F)

A#/Bb+
Augmented Triad

X X

3

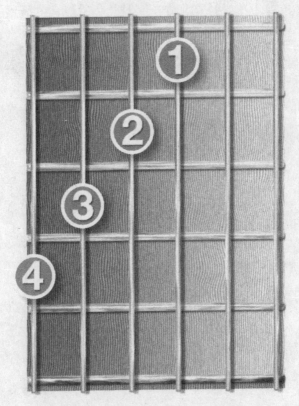

Chord Spelling
1st (Bb), 3rd (D), #5th (F#)

A♯/B♭°
Diminished Triad

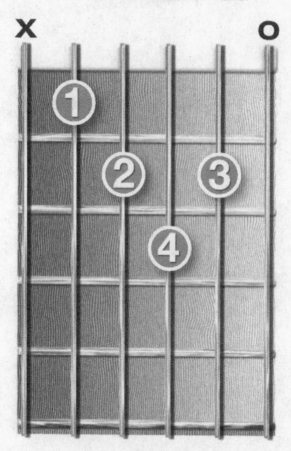

Chord Spelling
1st (B♭), ♭3rd (D♭), ♭5th (F♭)

A♯/B♭sus2
Suspended 2nd

Chord Spelling
1st (B♭), 2nd (C), 5th (F)

Online access
flametreemusic.com

Scan the code
to hear the chord

A♯/B♭sus4
Suspended 4th

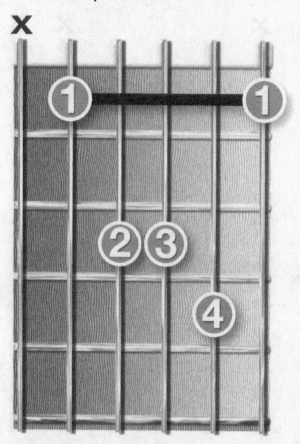

Chord Spelling

1st (B♭), 4th (E♭), 5th (F)

A#/B♭5
5th (Power Chord)

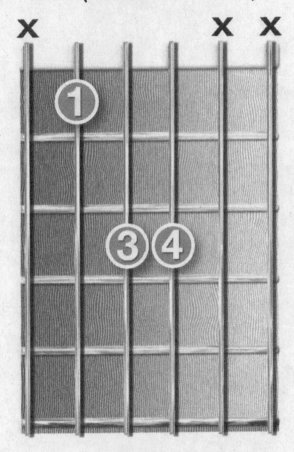

Chord Spelling
1st (B♭), 5th (F)

A♯/B♭6
Major 6th

X

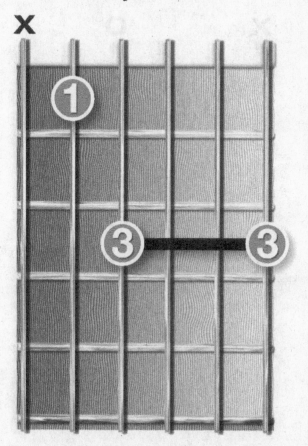

Chord Spelling
1st (B♭), 3rd (D), 5th (F), 6th (G)

A♯/B♭m6
Minor 6th

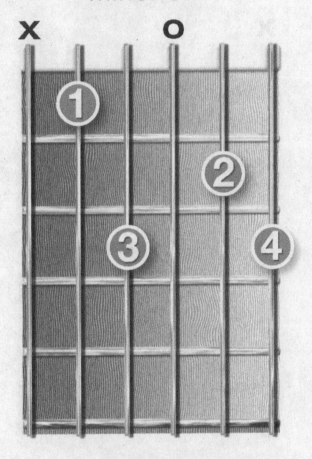

Chord Spelling

1st (B♭), ♭3rd (D♭), 5th (F), 6th (G)

A♯/B♭6sus4
6th Suspended 4th

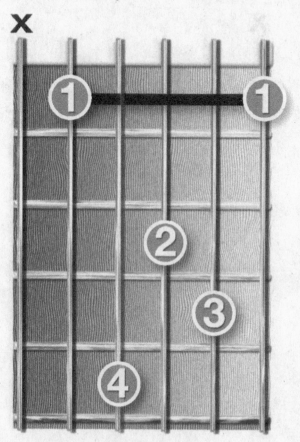

Chord Spelling
1st (B♭), 4th (E♭), 5th (F), 6th (G)

Online access
flametreemusic.com Scan the code
to hear the chord

45

A#/B♭maj7
Major 7th

Chord Spelling
1st (B♭), 3rd (D), 5th (F), 7th (A)

A#/B♭m7
Minor 7th

Chord Spelling
1st (B♭), ♭3rd (D♭), 5th (F), ♭7th (A♭)

A♯/B♭7
Dominant 7th

Chord Spelling
1st (B♭), 3rd (D), 5th (F), ♭7th (A♭)

A♯/B♭°7
Diminished 7th

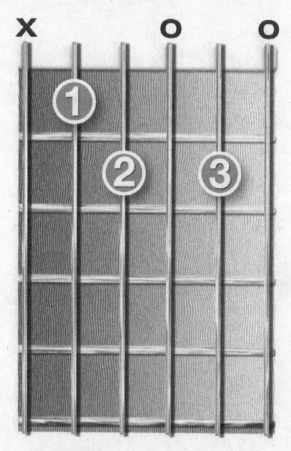

Chord Spelling
1st (B♭), ♭3rd (D♭), ♭5th (F♭), ♭♭7th (A♭♭)

A#/B♭7sus4
Dominant 7th Suspended 4th

Chord Spelling
1st (B♭), 4th (E♭), 5th (F), ♭7th (A♭)

A♯/B♭maj9
Major 9th

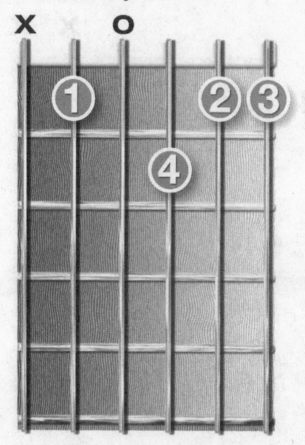

Chord Spelling
1st (B♭), 3rd (D), 5th (F), 7th (A), 9th (C)

Online access
flametreemusic.com

Scan the code
to hear the chord

51

A#/B♭m9
Minor 9th

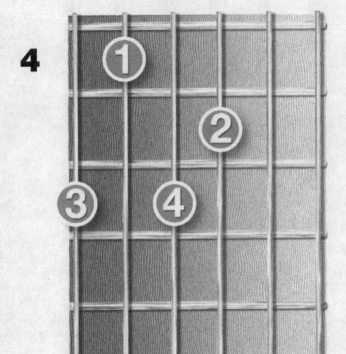

Chord Spelling
1st (B♭), ♭3rd (D♭), 5th (F), ♭7th (A♭), 9th (C)

A♯/B♭9
Dominant 9th

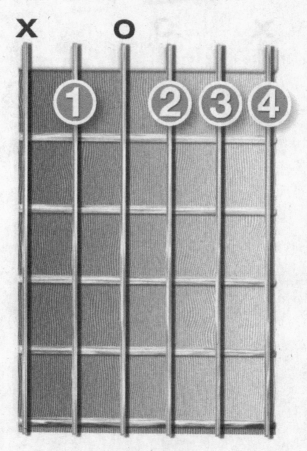

Chord Spelling
1st (B♭), 3rd (D), 5th (F), ♭7th (A♭), 9th (C)

A♯/B♭maj11
Major 11th

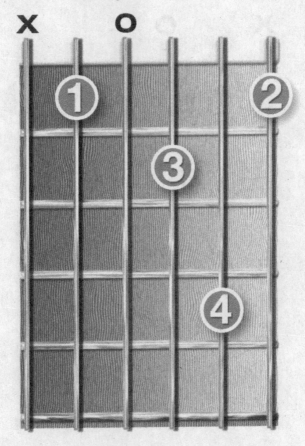

Chord Spelling
1st (B♭), 3rd (D), 5th (F), 7th (A), 9th (C), 11th (E♭)

Online access
flametreemusic.com Scan the code
to hear the chord

A♯/B♭maj13
Major 13th

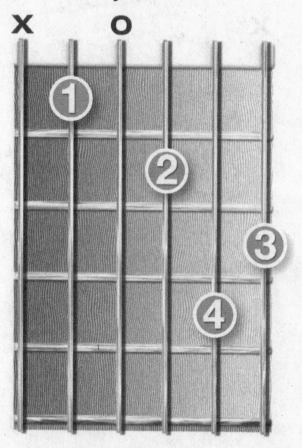

Chord Spelling
1st (B♭), 3rd (D), 5th (F), 7th (A), 9th (C), 11th (E♭), 13th (G)

Online access
flametreemusic.com

Scan the code
to hear the chord

B
Major

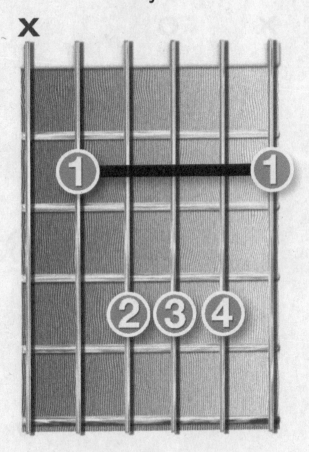

Chord Spelling
1st (B), 3rd (D♯), 5th (F♯)

Bm
Minor

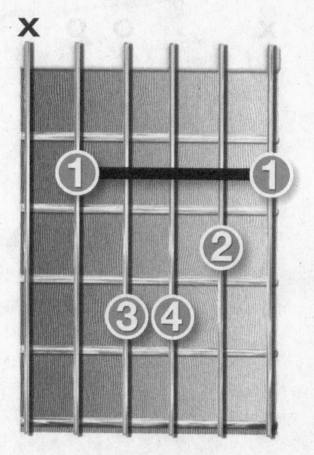

Chord Spelling
1st (B), ♭3rd (D), 5th (F♯)

B+
Augmented Triad

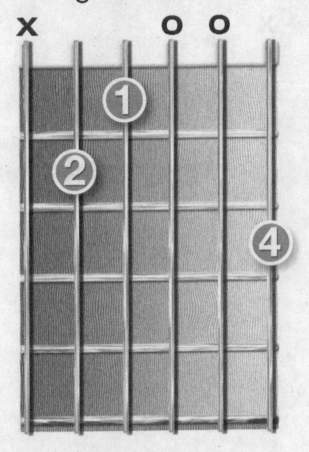

Chord Spelling

1st (B), 3rd (D♯), ♯5th (Fx)

Online access
flametreemusic.com

Scan the code
to hear the chord

B°
Diminished Triad

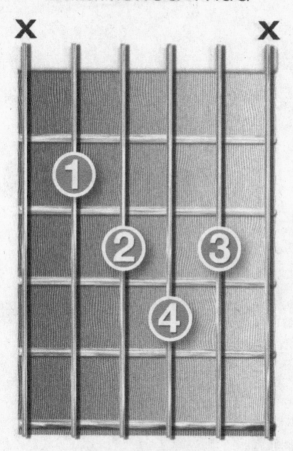

Chord Spelling

1st (B), ♭3rd (D), ♭5th (F)

Bsus2
Suspended 2nd

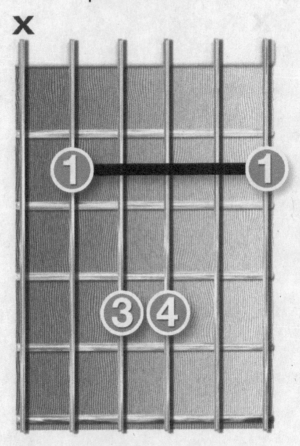

Chord Spelling

1st (B), 2nd (C#), 5th (F#)

Bsus4
Suspended 4th

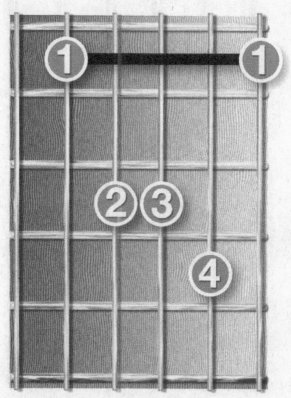

Chord Spelling
1st (B), 4th (E), 5th (F♯)

Online access
flametreemusic.com

Scan the code
to hear the chord

B5
5th (Power Chord)

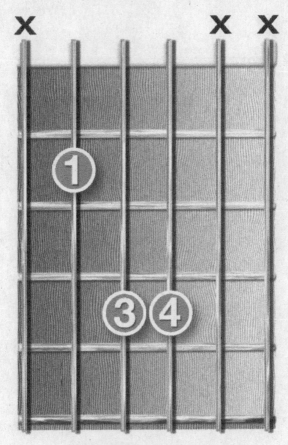

Chord Spelling
1st (B), 5th (F♯)

Online access
flametreemusic.com
 Scan the code
to hear the chord

B6
Major 6th

Chord Spelling
1st (B), 3rd (D#), 5th (F#), 6th (G#)

Online access
flametreemusic.com Scan the code
to hear the chord

Bm6
Minor 6th

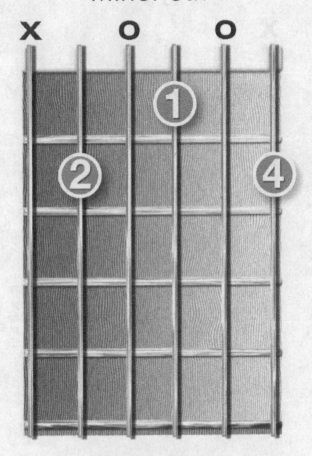

Chord Spelling
1st (B), ♭3rd (D), 5th (F♯), 6th (G♯)

B6sus4
6th Suspended 4th

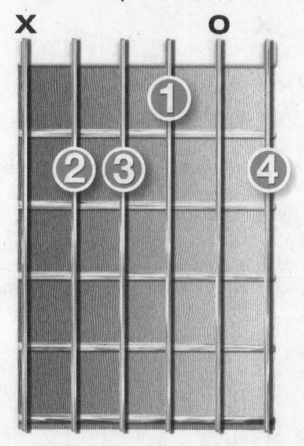

Chord Spelling
1st (B), 4th (E), 5th (F♯), 6th (G♯)

Bmaj7
Major 7th

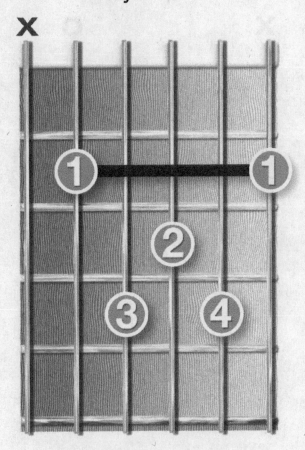

Chord Spelling
1st (B), 3rd (D♯), 5th (F♯), 7th (A♯)

Online access
flametreemusic.com

Scan the code
to hear the chord

Bm7
Minor 7th

Chord Spelling
1st (B), ♭3rd (D), 5th (F♯), ♭7th (A)

B7
Dominant 7th

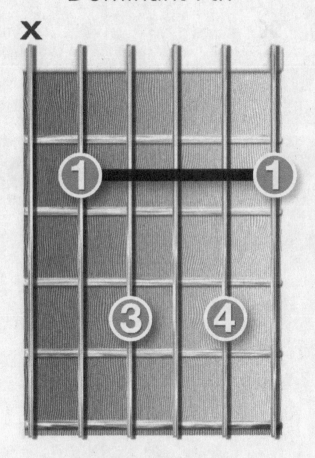

Chord Spelling
1st (B), 3rd (D♯), 5th (F♯), ♭7th (A)

Online access
flametreemusic.com

Scan the code
to hear the chord

B°7
Diminished 7th

Chord Spelling

1st (B), ♭3rd (D), ♭5th (F), ♭♭7th (A♭)

B7sus4

Dominant 7th Suspended 4th

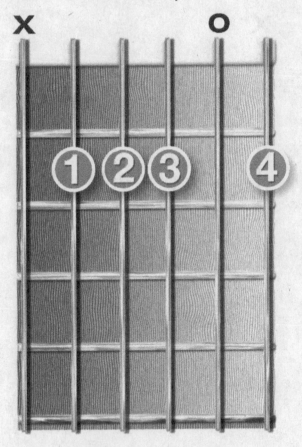

Chord Spelling

1st (B), 4th (E), 5th (F♯), ♭7th (A)

Bmaj9
Major 9th

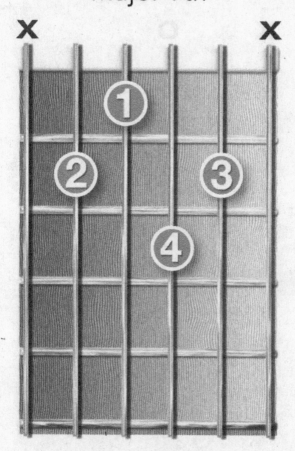

Chord Spelling

1st (B), 3rd (D♯), 5th (F♯), 7th (A♯), 9th (C♯)

Online access
flametreemusic.com

Scan the code
to hear the chord

Bm9
Minor 9th

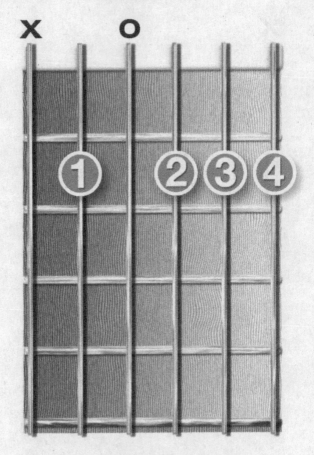

Chord Spelling
1st (B), ♭3rd (D), 5th (F♯), ♭7th (A), 9th (C♯)

Online access
flametreemusic.com

Scan the code
to hear the chord

B9
Dominant 9th

Chord Spelling
1st (B), 3rd (D♯), 5th (F♯), ♭7th (A), 9th (C♯)

Bmaj11
Major 11th

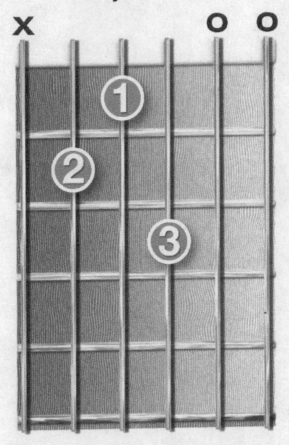

Chord Spelling

1st (B), 3rd (D♯), 5th (F♯), 7th (A♯), 9th (C♯), 11th (E)

Online access
flametreemusic.com

Scan the code
to hear the chord

Bmaj13
Major 13th

Chord Spelling
1st (B), 3rd (D#), 5th (F#), 7th (A#), 9th (C#), 11th (E), 13th (G#)

C
Major

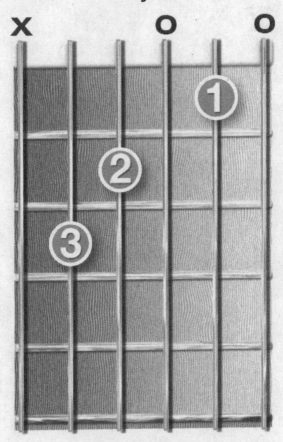

Chord Spelling
1st (C), 3rd (E), 5th (G)

Cm
Minor

X

3

Chord Spelling
1st (C), ♭3rd (E♭), 5th (G)

C+

Augmented Triad

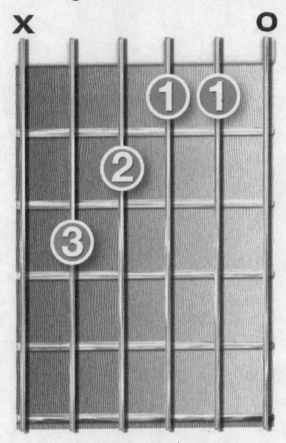

Chord Spelling

1st (C), 3rd (E), #5th (G#)

Online access
flametreemusic.com

Scan the code
to hear the chord

C°
Diminished Triad

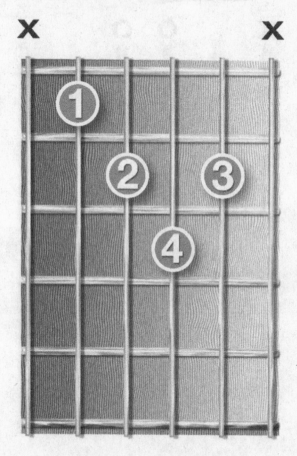

Chord Spelling

1st (C), ♭3rd (E♭), ♭5th (G♭)

Online access
flametreemusic.com

Scan the code
to hear the chord

Csus2
Suspended 2nd

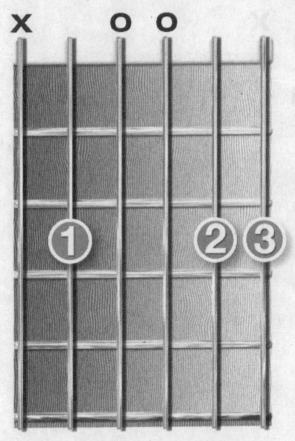

Chord Spelling
1st (C), 2nd (D), 5th (G)

Online access
flametreemusic.com

Scan the code
to hear the chord

Csus4
Suspended 4th

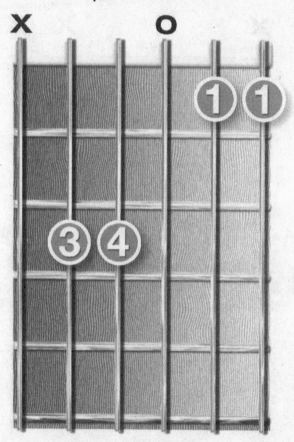

Chord Spelling
1st (C), 4th (F), 5th (G)

Online access
flametreemusic.com

Scan the code
to hear the chord

C5
5th (Power Chord)

Chord Spelling

1st (C), 5th (G)

C6
Major 6th

Chord Spelling
1st (C), 3rd (E), 5th (G), 6th (A)

Cm6
Minor 6th

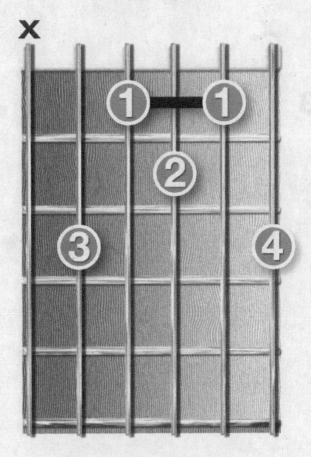

Chord Spelling
1st (C), ♭3rd (E♭), 5th (G), 6th (A)

Online access
flametreemusic.com

Scan the code
to hear the chord

C6sus4
6th Suspended 4th

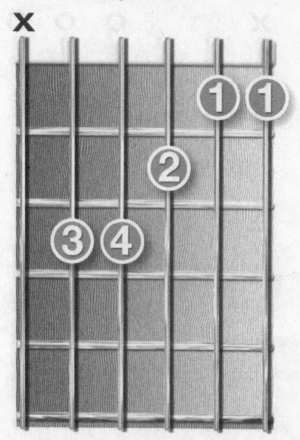

Chord Spelling
1st (C), 4th (F), 5th (G), 6th (A)

Online access
flametreemusic.com

Scan the code
to hear the chord

Cmaj7
Major 7th

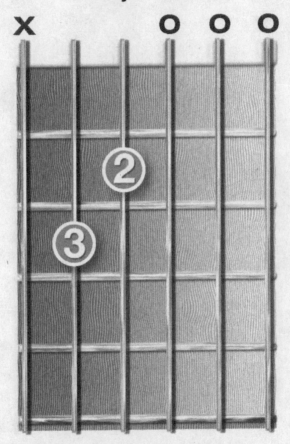

Chord Spelling
1st (C), 3rd (E), 5th (G), 7th (B)

Online access
flametreemusic.com

Scan the code
to hear the chord

Cm7
Minor 7th

Chord Spelling
1st (C), ♭3rd (E♭), 5th (G), ♭7th (B♭)

C7
Dominant 7th

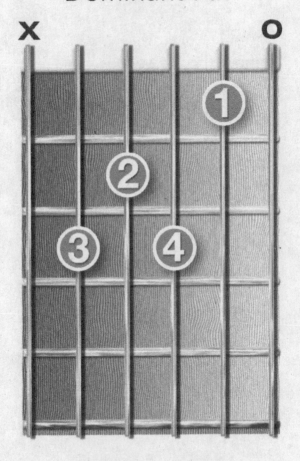

Chord Spelling
1st (C), 3rd (E), 5th (G), ♭7th (B♭)

C°7
Diminished 7th

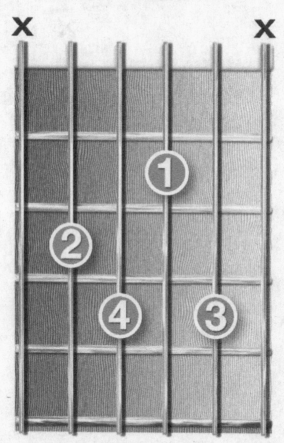

Chord Spelling

1st (C), ♭3rd (E♭), ♭5th (G♭), ♭♭7th (B♭♭)

C7sus4
Dominant 7th Suspended 4th

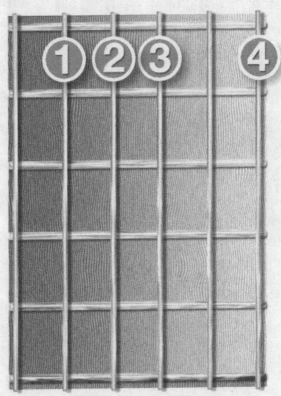

Chord Spelling
1st (C), 4th (F), 5th (G), ♭7th (B♭)

Cmaj9
Major 9th

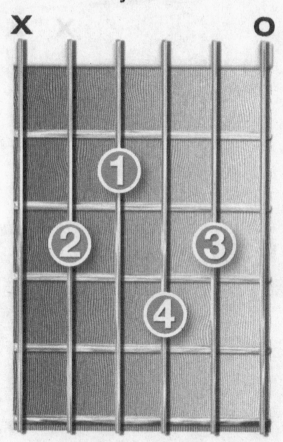

Chord Spelling
1st (C), 3rd (E), 5th (G), 7th (B), 9th (D)

Cm9
Minor 9th

Chord Spelling
1st (C), ♭3rd (E♭), 5th (G), ♭7th (B♭), 9th (D)

Online access
flametreemusic.com

Scan the code
to hear the chord

C9
Dominant 9th

Chord Spelling
1st (C), 3rd (E), 5th (G), ♭7th (B♭), 9th (D)

Cmaj11
Major 11th

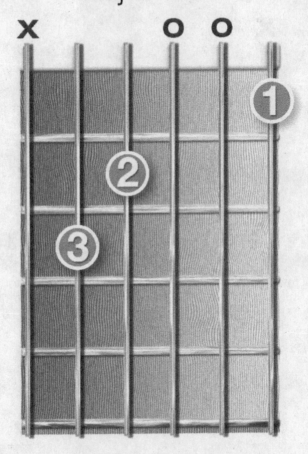

Chord Spelling
1st (C), 3rd (E), 5th (G), 7th (B), 9th (D), 11th (F)

Online access
flametreemusic.com

Scan the code
to hear the chord

Cmaj13
Major 13th

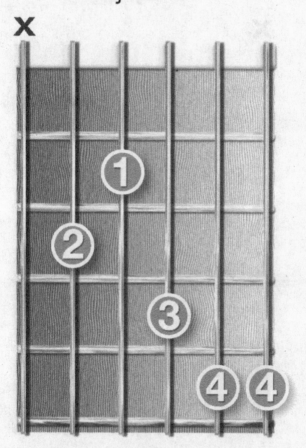

Chord Spelling
1st (C), 3rd (E), 5th (G), 7th (B), 9th (D), 11th (F), 13th (A)

C#/D♭
Major

Chord Spelling
1st (C#), 3rd (E#), 5th (G#)

Online access
flametreemusic.com

Scan the code
to hear the chord

96

C♯/D♭m
Minor

Chord Spelling
1st (C♯), ♭3rd (E), 5th (G♯)

C#/D♭+
Augmented Triad

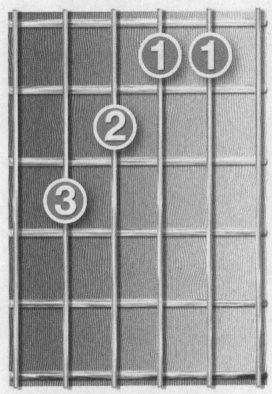

Chord Spelling
1st (C#), 3rd (E#), #5th (Gx)

C#/D♭°
Diminished Triad

X   O

4

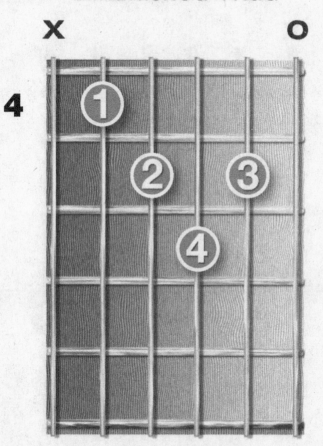

Chord Spelling

1st (C#), ♭3rd (E), ♭5th (G)

C#/D♭sus2
Suspended 2nd

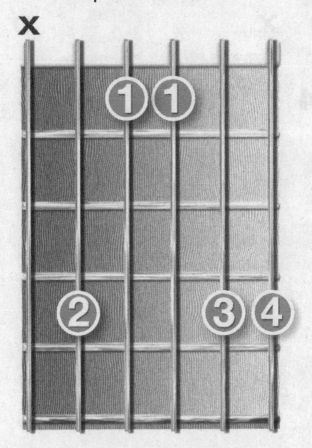

Chord Spelling
1st (C#), 2nd (D#), 5th (G#)

C#/D♭sus4
Suspended 4th

Chord Spelling
1st (C#), 4th (F#), 5th (G#)

C#/D♭5
5th (Power Chord)

Chord Spelling
1st (C#), 5th (G#)

C#/D♭6
Major 6th

X

4

Chord Spelling
1st (C#), 3rd (E#), 5th (G#), 6th (A#)

C#/D♭m6
Minor 6th

Chord Spelling
1st (C#), ♭3rd (E), 5th (G#), 6th (A#)

C#/D♭6sus4
6th Suspended 4th

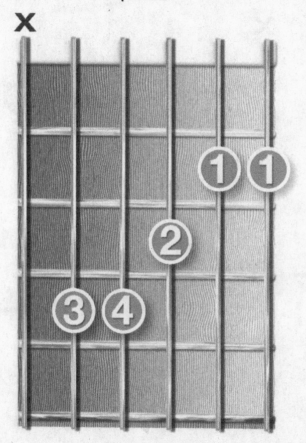

Chord Spelling
1st (C#), 4th (F#), 5th (G#), 6th (A#)

C#/D♭maj7
Major 7th

Chord Spelling

1st (C#), 3rd (E#), 5th (G#), 7th (B#)

Online access
flametreemusic.com

Scan the code
to hear the chord

C#/D♭m7
Minor 7th

X

2

Chord Spelling
1st (C#), ♭3rd (E), 5th (G#), ♭7th (B)

C#/D♭7
Dominant 7th

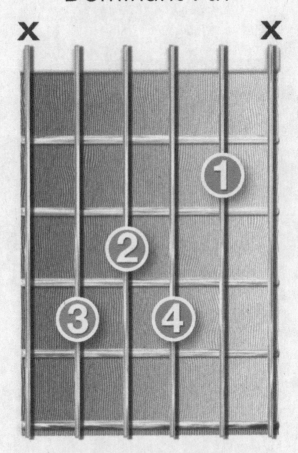

Chord Spelling
1st (C#), 3rd (E#), 5th (G#), ♭7th (B)

C#/D♭°7
Diminished 7th

Chord Spelling
1st (C#), ♭3rd (E), ♭5th (G), ♭♭7th (B♭)

C♯/D♭7sus4
Dominant 7th Suspended 4th

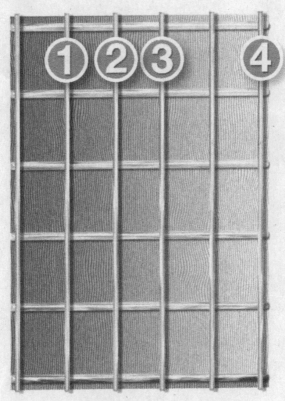

Chord Spelling

1st (C♯), 4th (F♯), 5th (G♯), ♭7th (B)

C#/D♭maj9
Major 9th

Chord Spelling
1st (C#), 3rd (E#), 5th (G#), 7th (B#), 9th (D#)

C#/D♭m9
Minor 9th

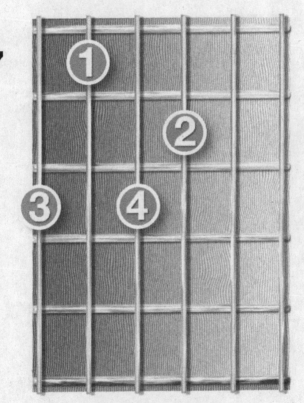

Chord Spelling
1st (C#), ♭3rd (E), 5th (G#), ♭7th (B), 9th (D#)

C#/D♭9
Dominant 9th

X

3

Chord Spelling
1st (C#), 3rd (E#), 5th (G#), ♭7th (B), 9th (D#)

C#/D♭maj11
Major 11th

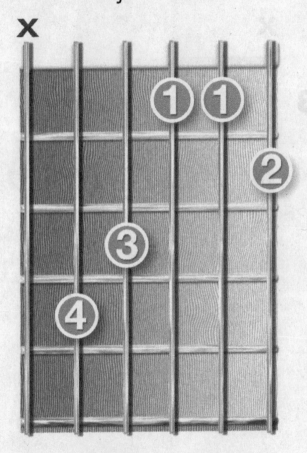

Chord Spelling

1st (C#), 3rd (E#), 5th (G#), 7th (B#), 9th (D#), 11th (F#)

Online access
flametreemusic.com

Scan the code
to hear the chord

C#/D♭maj13
Major 13th

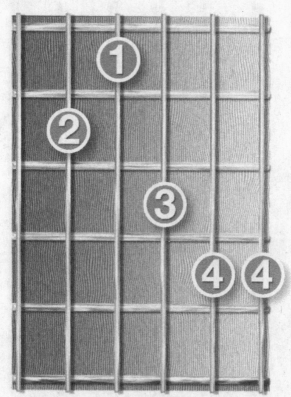

Chord Spelling
1st (C#), 3rd (E#), 5th (G#), 7th (B#), 9th (D#), 11th (F#), 13th (A#)

Online access
flametreemusic.com

Scan the code
to hear the chord

D
Major

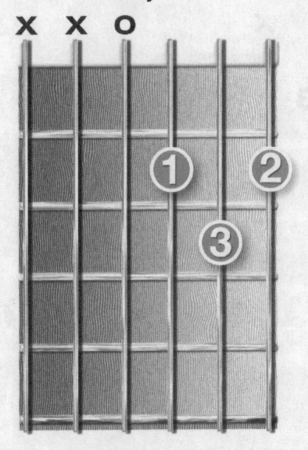

Chord Spelling

1st (D), 3rd (F♯), 5th (A)

Dm
Minor

X   X   O

Chord Spelling
1st (D), ♭3rd (F), 5th (A)

Online access
flametreemusic.com

Scan the code
to hear the chord

D+
Augmented Triad

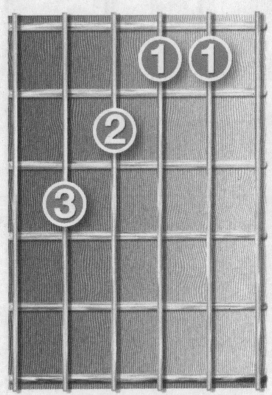

Chord Spelling
1st (D), 3rd (F#), #5th (A#)

D°
Diminished Triad

Chord Spelling
1st (D), ♭3rd (F), ♭5th (A♭)

Online access
flametreemusic.com

Scan the code
to hear the chord

Dsus2
Suspended 2nd

X X O   O

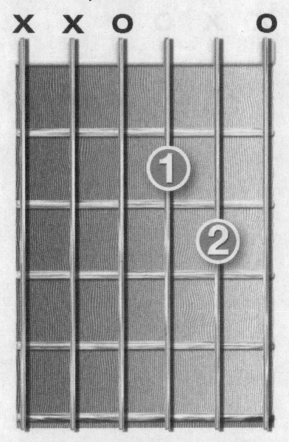

Chord Spelling
1st (D), 2nd (E), 5th (A)

Online access
flametreemusic.com Scan the code
to hear the chord

Dsus4
Suspended 4th

X X O

Chord Spelling
1st (D), 4th (G), 5th (A)

D5
5th (Power Chord)

X X O   X

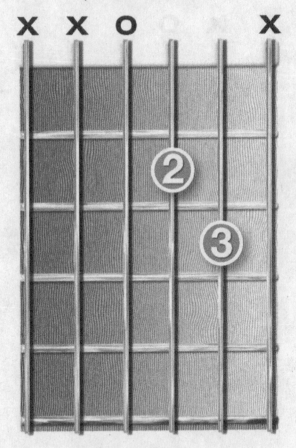

Chord Spelling
1st (D), 5th (A)

D6
Major 6th

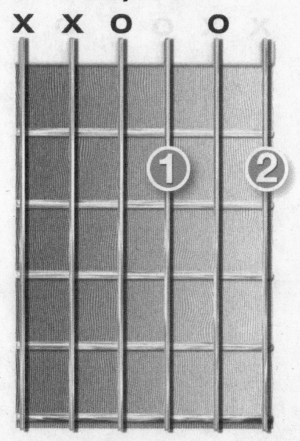

Chord Spelling
1st (D), 3rd (F#), 5th (A), 6th (B)

Dm6
Minor 6th

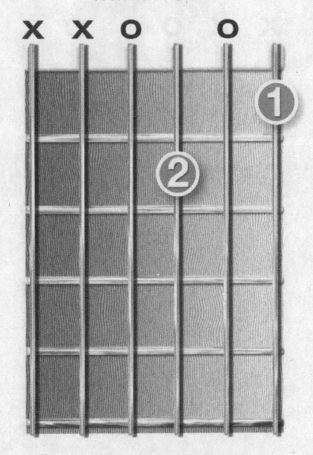

Chord Spelling
1st (D), ♭3rd (F), 5th (A), 6th (B)

Online access
flametreemusic.com

Scan the code
to hear the chord

D6sus4
6th Suspended 4th

Chord Spelling
1st (D), 4th (G), 5th (A), 6th (B)

Dmaj7
Major 7th

Chord Spelling
1st (D), 3rd (F♯), 5th (A), 7th (C♯)

Online access
flametreemusic.com

Scan the code
to hear the chord

Dm7

Minor 7th

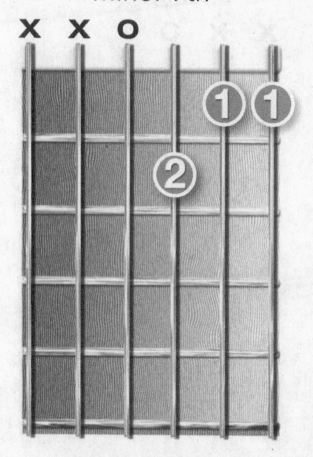

Chord Spelling

1st (D), ♭3rd (F), 5th (A), ♭7th (C)

Online access
flametreemusic.com

**Scan the code
to hear the chord**

D7
Dominant 7th

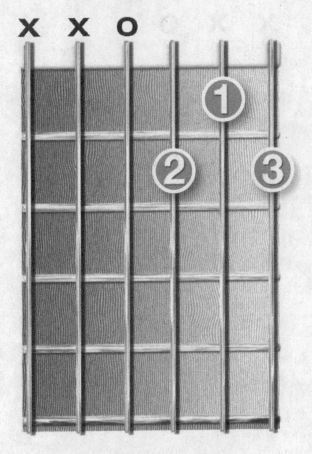

Chord Spelling
1st (D), 3rd (F#), 5th (A), ♭7th (C)

D°7
Diminished 7th

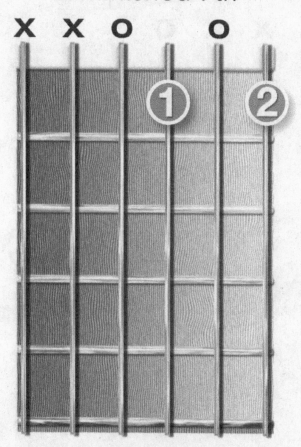

Chord Spelling
1st (D), ♭3rd (F), ♭5th (A♭), ♭♭7th (B)

D7sus4
Dominant 7th Suspended 4th

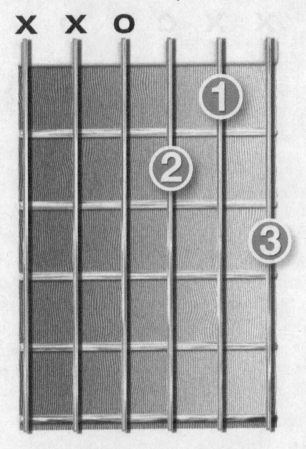

Chord Spelling
1st (D), 4th (G), 5th (A), ♭7th (C)

Online access
flametreemusic.com Scan the code
to hear the chord

Dmaj9
Major 9th

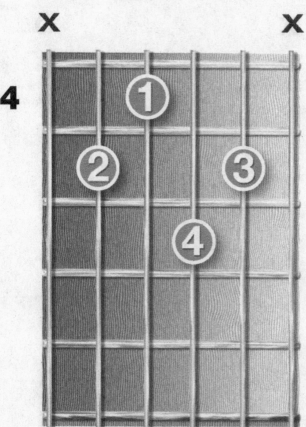

Chord Spelling
1st (D), 3rd (F♯), 5th (A), 7th (C♯), 9th (E)

Online access
flametreemusic.com Scan the code
to hear the chord

Dm9
Minor 9th

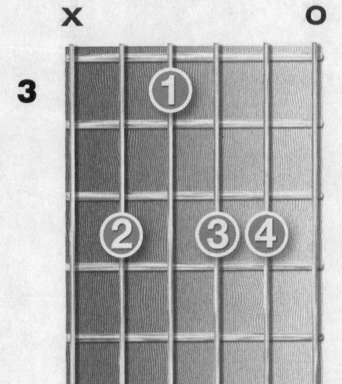

Chord Spelling

1st (D), ♭3rd (F), 5th (A), ♭7th (C), 9th (E)

Online access
flametreemusic.com

Scan the code
to hear the chord

D9
Dominant 9th

Chord Spelling
1st (D), 3rd (F♯), 5th (A), ♭7th (C), 9th (E)

Online access
flametreemusic.com

Scan the code
to hear the chord

Dmaj11
Major 11th

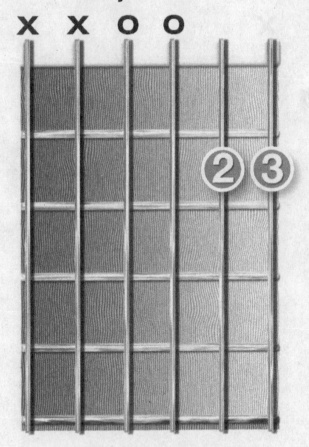

Chord Spelling
1st (D), 3rd (F#), 5th (A), 7th (C#), 9th (E), 11th (G)

Dmaj13
Major 13th

X

4

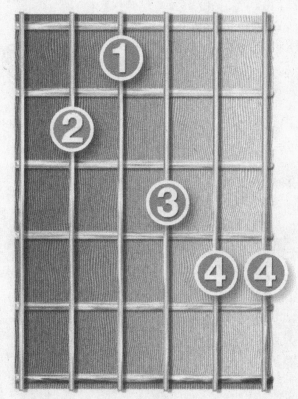

Chord Spelling
1st (D), 3rd (F#), 5th (A), 7th (C#), 9th (E), 11th (G), 13th (B)

Online access
flametreemusic.com

Scan the code
to hear the chord

D#/E♭
Major

Chord Spelling
1st (E♭), 3rd (G), 5th (B♭)

D#/E♭m
Minor

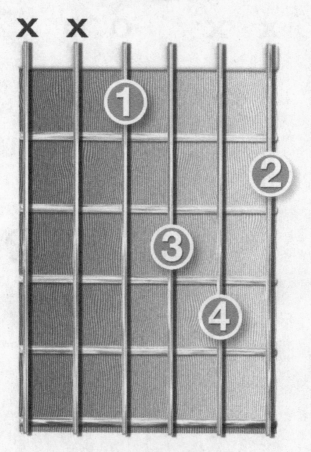

Chord Spelling
1st (E♭), ♭3rd (G♭), 5th (B♭)

D#/E♭+
Augmented Triad

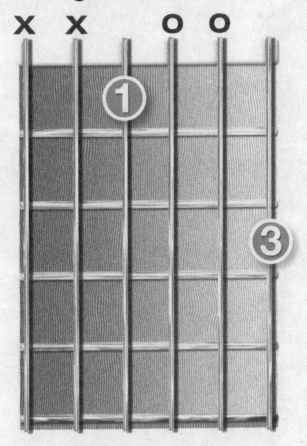

Chord Spelling
1st (E♭), 3rd (G), #5th (B)

D♯/E♭°
Diminished Triad

Chord Spelling
1st (E♭), ♭3rd (G♭), ♭5th (B♭♭)

D#/E♭sus2
Suspended 2nd

Chord Spelling

1st (E♭), 2nd (F), 5th (B♭)

Online access
flametreemusic.com Scan the code
to hear the chord

D#/E♭sus4
Suspended 4th

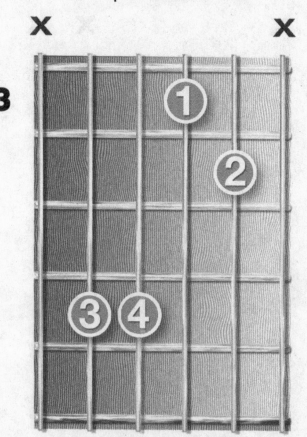

Chord Spelling
1st (E♭), 4th (A♭), 5th (B♭)

Online access
flametreemusic.com

Scan the code
to hear the chord

D♯/E♭5
5th (Power Chord)

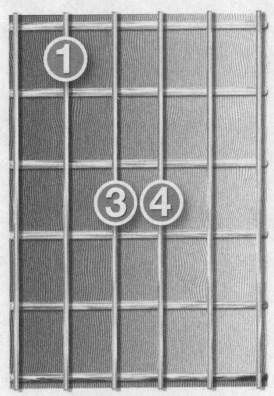

Chord Spelling

1st (E♭), 5th (B♭)

Online access
flametreemusic.com

Scan the code
to hear the chord

D#/E♭6
Major 6th

X X

Chord Spelling
1st (E♭), 3rd (G), 5th (B♭), 6th (C)

D#/E♭m6
Minor 6th

Chord Spelling
1st (E♭), ♭3rd (G♭), 5th (B♭), 6th (C)

D♯/E♭6sus4
6th Suspended 4th

Chord Spelling
1st (E♭), 4th (A♭), 5th (B♭), 6th (C)

D#/E♭maj7
Major 7th

Chord Spelling
1st (E♭), 3rd (G), 5th (B♭), 7th (D)

D♯/E♭m7
Minor 7th

Chord Spelling
1st (E♭), ♭3rd (G♭), 5th (B♭), ♭7th (D♭)

Online access
flametreemusic.com

Scan the code
to hear the chord

D#/E♭7
Dominant 7th

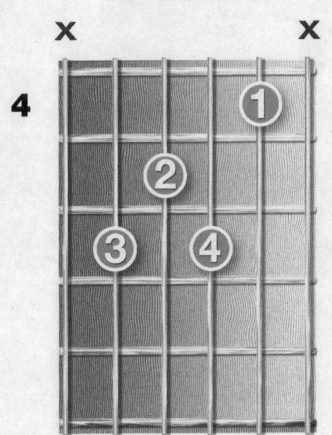

Chord Spelling
1st (E♭), 3rd (G), 5th (B♭), ♭7th (D♭)

D♯/E♭°7
Diminished 7th

Chord Spelling
1st (E♭), ♭3rd (G♭), ♭5th (B♭♭), ♭♭7th (D♭♭)

D♯/E♭7sus4
Dominant 7th Suspended 4th

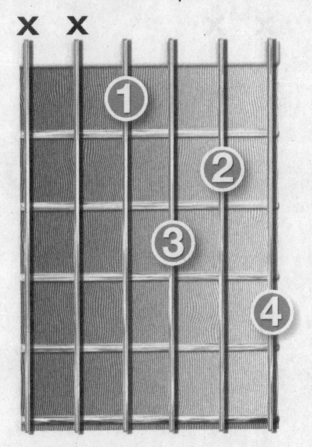

Chord Spelling
1st (E♭), 4th (A♭), 5th (B♭), ♭7th (D♭)

D♯/E♭maj9
Major 9th

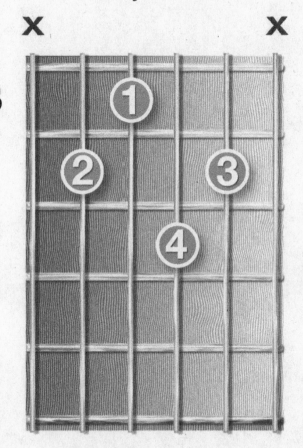

Chord Spelling
1st (E♭), 3rd (G), 5th (B♭), 7th (D), 9th (F)

Online access
flametreemusic.com

Scan the code
to hear the chord

D#/E♭m9
Minor 9th

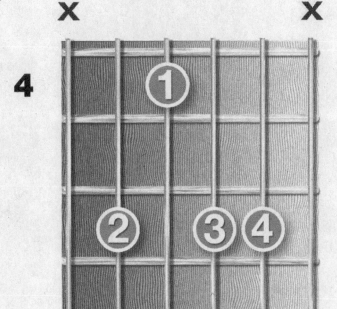

X   X

4

① ② ③ ④

Chord Spelling
1st (E♭), ♭3rd (G♭), 5th (B♭), ♭7th (D♭), 9th (F)

Online access
flametreemusic.com

Scan the code
to hear the chord

D♯/E♭9
Dominant 9th

Chord Spelling
1st (E♭), 3rd (G), 5th (B♭), ♭7th (D♭), 9th (F)

D#/E♭maj11
Major 11th

Chord Spelling

1st (E♭), 3rd (G), 5th (B♭), 7th (D), 9th (F), 11th (A♭)

D♯/E♭maj13
Major 13th

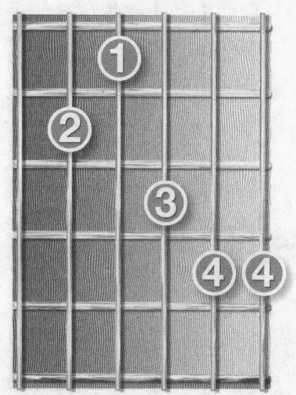

X

5

Chord Spelling
1st (E♭), 3rd (G), 5th (B♭), 7th (D), 9th (F), 11th (A♭), 13th (C)

E
Major

Chord Spelling
1st (E), 3rd (G♯), 5th (B)

Online access
flametreemusic.com Scan the code
to hear the chord

Em
Minor

Chord Spelling
1st (E), ♭3rd (G), 5th (B)

Online access
flametreemusic.com

Scan the code
to hear the chord

E+
Augmented Triad

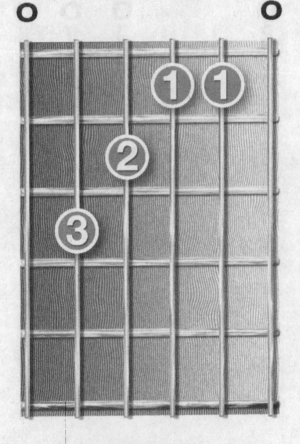

5

Chord Spelling
1st (E), 3rd (G♯), ♯5th (B♯)

Online access
flametreemusic.com

Scan the code
to hear the chord

E°
Diminished Triad

Chord Spelling
1st (E), ♭3rd (G), ♭5th (B♭)

Online access
flametreemusic.com Scan the code
to hear the chord

Esus2
Suspended 2nd

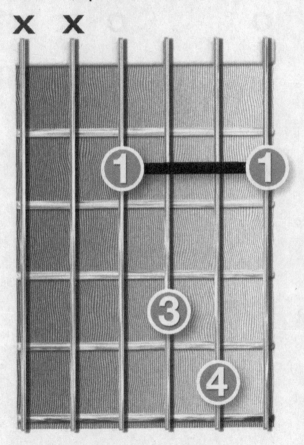

Chord Spelling
1st (E), 2nd (F#), 5th (B)

Online access
flametreemusic.com

Scan the code
to hear the chord

Esus4
Suspended 4th

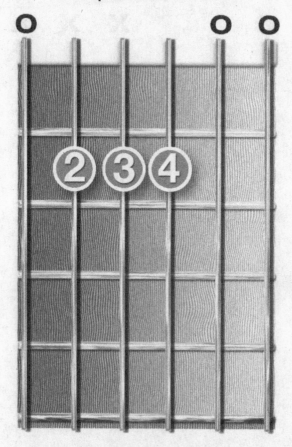

Chord Spelling
1st (E), 4th (A), 5th (B)

Online access
flametreemusic.com

Scan the code
to hear the chord

E5
5th (Power Chord)

Chord Spelling
1st (E), 5th (B)

Online access
flametreemusic.com Scan the code
to hear the chord

E6
Major 6th

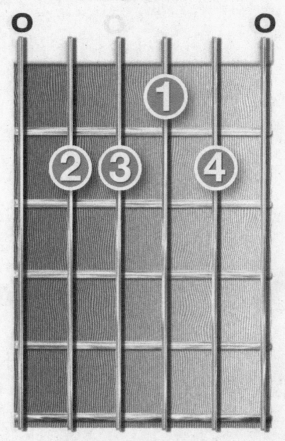

Chord Spelling
1st (E), 3rd (G♯), 5th (B), 6th (C♯)

Online access
flametreemusic.com

Scan the code
to hear the chord

Em6
Minor 6th

Chord Spelling
1st (E), ♭3rd (G), 5th (B), 6th (C♯)

Online access
flametreemusic.com

Scan the code
to hear the chord

E6sus4
6th Suspended 4th

Chord Spelling
1st (E), 4th (A), 5th (B), 6th (C#)

Emaj7
Major 7th

Chord Spelling
1st (E), 3rd (G#), 5th (B), 7th (D#)

Online access
flametreemusic.com

Scan the code
to hear the chord

Em7
Minor 7th

Chord Spelling
1st (E), ♭3rd (G), 5th (B), ♭7th (D)

E7
Dominant 7th

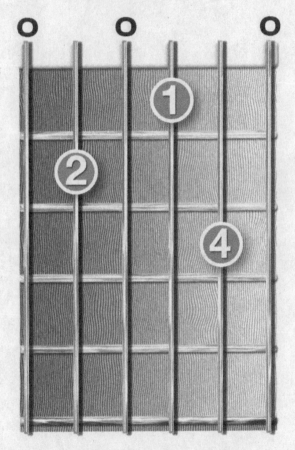

Chord Spelling
1st (E), 3rd (G#), 5th (B), ♭7th (D)

E°7
Diminished 7th

Chord Spelling

1st (E), ♭3rd (G), ♭5th (B♭), ♭♭7th (D♭)

Online access
flametreemusic.com

Scan the code
to hear the chord

E7sus4
Dominant 7th Suspended 4th

Chord Spelling
1st (E), 4th (A), 5th (B), ♭7th (D)

Emaj9
Major 9th

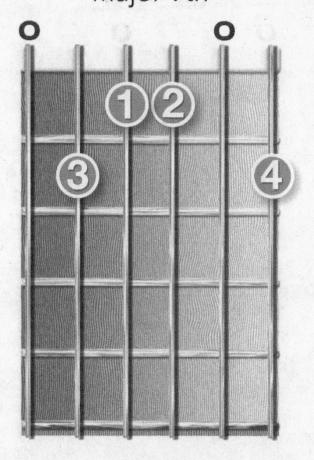

Chord Spelling
1st (E), 3rd (G#), 5th (B), 7th (D#), 9th (F#)

Online access
flametreemusic.com Scan the code
to hear the chord

Em9
Minor 9th

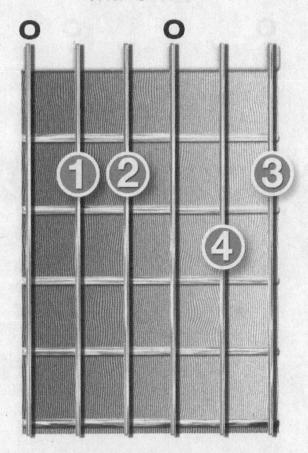

Chord Spelling
1st (E), ♭3rd (G), 5th (B), ♭7th (D), 9th (F♯)

Online access
flametreemusic.com

Scan the code
to hear the chord

E9
Dominant 9th

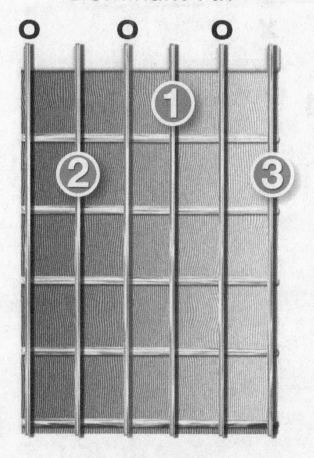

Chord Spelling

1st (E), 3rd (G♯), 5th (B), ♭7th (D), 9th (F♯)

Emaj11
Major 11th

4

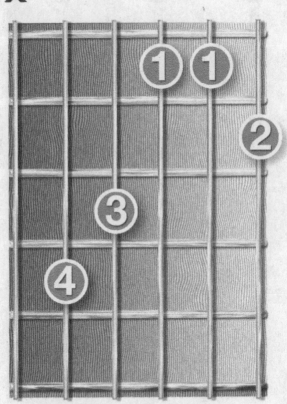

Chord Spelling
1st (E), 3rd (G♯), 5th (B), 7th (D♯), 9th (F♯), 11th (A)

Emaj13
Major 13th

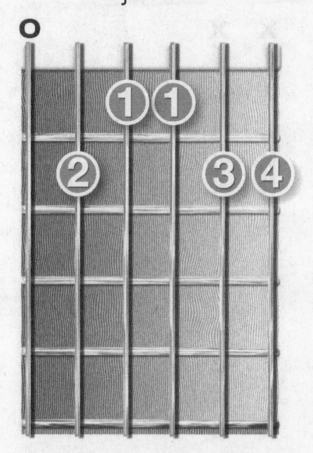

Chord Spelling
1st (E), 3rd (G♯), 5th (B), 7th (D♯), 9th (F), 11th (A), 13th (C♯)

F
Major

Chord Spelling
1st (F), 3rd (A), 5th (C)

Fm
Minor

Chord Spelling
1st (F), ♭3rd (A♭), 5th (C)

F+
Augmented Triad

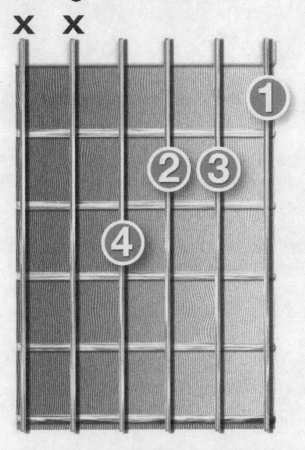

Chord Spelling
1st (F), 3rd (A), #5th (C#)

F°
Diminished Triad

Chord Spelling
1st (F), ♭3rd (A♭), ♭5th (C♭)

Online access
flametreemusic.com

Scan the code
to hear the chord

Fsus2
Suspended 2nd

Chord Spelling
1st (F), 2nd (G), 5th (C)

Online access
flametreemusic.com

Scan the code
to hear the chord

Fsus4
Suspended 4th

Chord Spelling
1st (F), 4th (B♭), 5th (C)

Online access
flametreemusic.com

Scan the code
to hear the chord

F5
5th (Power Chord)

Chord Spelling
1st (F), 5th (C)

Online access
flametreemusic.com

Scan the code
to hear the chord

F6
Major 6th

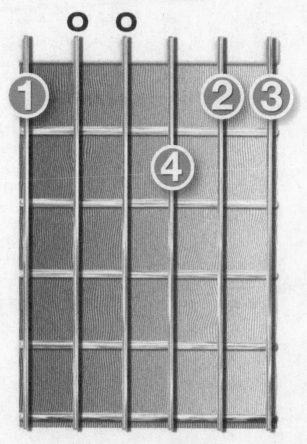

Chord Spelling
1st (F), 3rd (A), 5th (C), 6th (D)

Fm6
Minor 6th

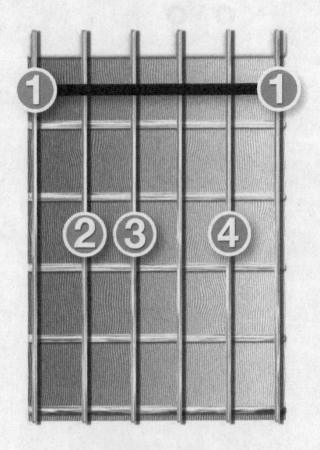

Chord Spelling
1st (F), ♭3rd (A♭), 5th (C), 6th (D)

F6sus4
6th Suspended 4th

Chord Spelling
1st (F), 4th (B♭), 5th (C), 6th (D)

Online access
flametreemusic.com

Scan the code
to hear the chord

Fmaj7
Major 7th

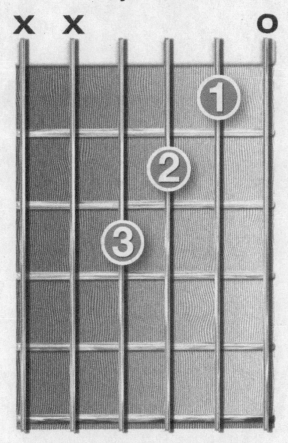

Chord Spelling

1st (F), 3rd (A), 5th (C), 7th (E)

Online access
flametreemusic.com

Scan the code
to hear the chord

Fm7
Minor 7th

Chord Spelling
1st (F), ♭3rd (A♭), 5th (C), ♭7th (E♭)

F7
Dominant 7th

Chord Spelling
1st (F), 3rd (A), 5th (C), ♭7th (E♭)

Online access
flametreemusic.com

Scan the code
to hear the chord

F°7
Diminished 7th

Chord Spelling
1st (F), ♭3rd (A♭), ♭5th (C♭), ♭♭7th (E♭♭)

F7sus4
Dominant 7th Suspended 4th

Chord Spelling
1st (F), 4th (B♭), 5th (C), ♭7th (E♭)

Online access
flametreemusic.com

Scan the code
to hear the chord

Fmaj9
Major 9th

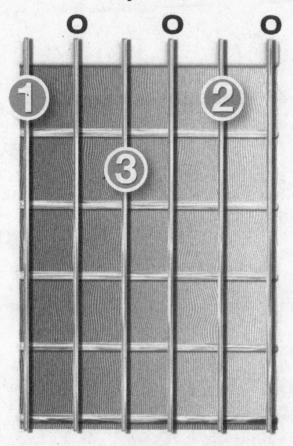

Chord Spelling
1st (F), 3rd (A), 5th (C), 7th (E), 9th (G)

Online access
flametreemusic.com

Scan the code
to hear the chord

Fm9
Minor 9th

Chord Spelling
1st (F), ♭3rd (A♭), 5th (C), ♭7th (E♭), 9th (G)

Online access
flametreemusic.com

Scan the code
to hear the chord

F9

Dominant 9th

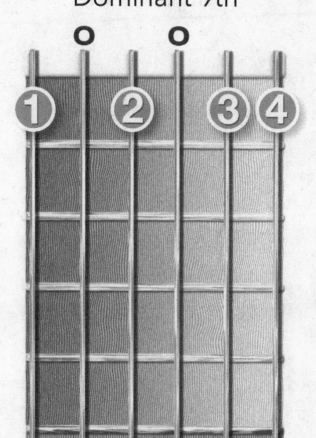

Chord Spelling

1st (F), 3rd (A), 5th (C), ♭7th (E♭), 9th (G)

Online access
flametreemusic.com

Scan the code
to hear the chord

Fmaj11
Major 11th

Chord Spelling

1st (F), 3rd (A), 5th (C), 7th (E), 9th (G), 11th (B♭)

Online access
flametreemusic.com

Scan the code
to hear the chord

Fmaj13
Major 13th

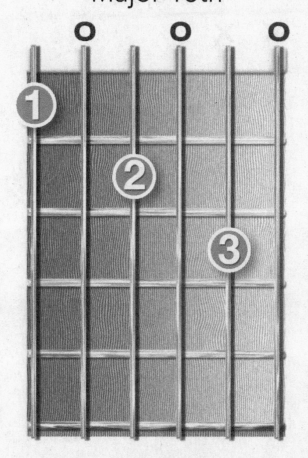

Chord Spelling

1st (F), 3rd (A), 5th (C), 7th (E), 9th (G), 11th (B♭), 13th (D)

Online access
flametreemusic.com

Scan the code
to hear the chord

F♯/G♭
Major

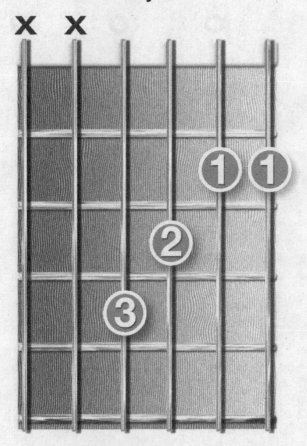

Chord Spelling
1st (F♯), 3rd (A♯), 5th (C♯)

F#/G♭m
Minor

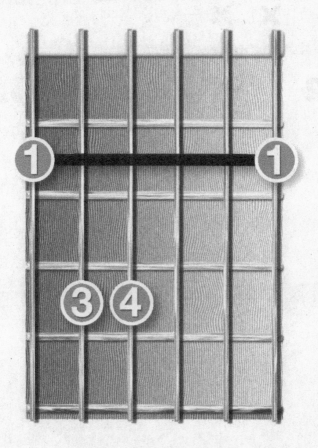

Chord Spelling
1st (F#), ♭3rd (A), 5th (C#)

F#/Gb+
Augmented Triad

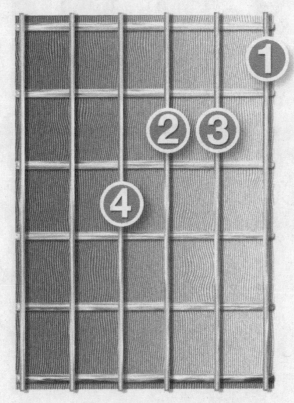

2

Chord Spelling
1st (F#), 3rd (A#), #5th (Cx)

Online access
flametreemusic.com

Scan the code
to hear the chord

F♯/G♭°
Diminished Triad

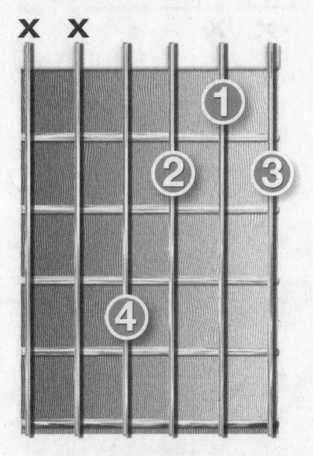

Chord Spelling
1st (F♯), ♭3rd (A), ♭5th (C)

F#/G♭sus2
Suspended 2nd

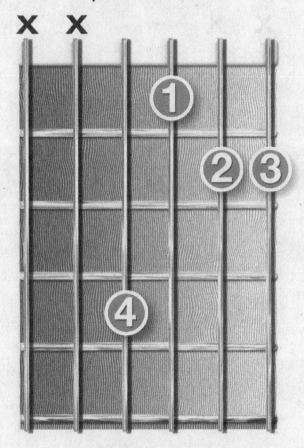

Chord Spelling
1st (F#), 2nd (G#), 5th (A#)

F♯/G♭sus4
Suspended 4th

Chord Spelling
1st (F♯), 4th (B), 5th (C♯)

Online access
flametreemusic.com Scan the code
to hear the chord

F#/G♭5
5th (Power Chord)

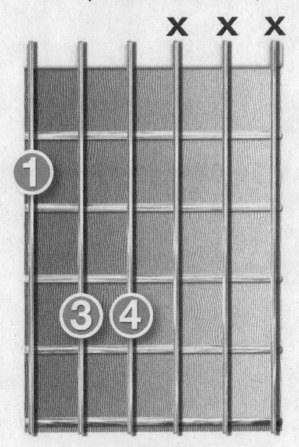

Chord Spelling
1st (F#), 5th (C#)

F#/G♭6
Major 6th

Chord Spelling
1st (F#), 3rd (A#), 5th (C#), 6th (D#)

F♯/G♭m6
Minor 6th

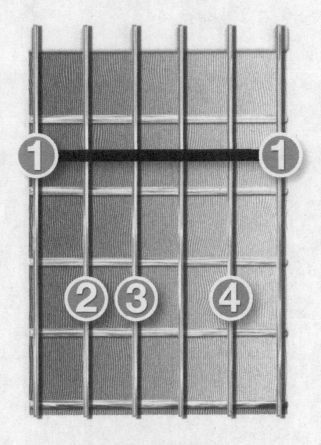

Chord Spelling
1st (F♯), ♭3rd (A), 5th (C♯), 6th (D♯)

Online access
flametreemusic.com

Scan the code
to hear the chord

F#/G♭6sus4
6th Suspended 4th

Chord Spelling
1st (F#), 4th (B), 5th (C#), 6th (D#)

F#/G♭maj7
Major 7th

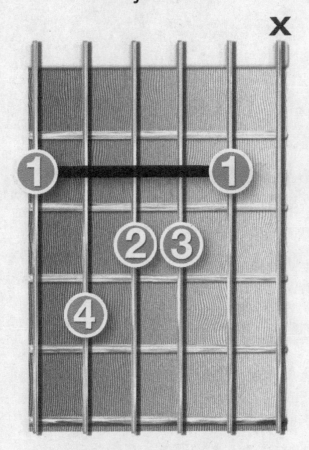

Chord Spelling
1st (F#), 3rd (A#), 5th (C#), 7th (F)

F#/G♭m7
Minor 7th

2

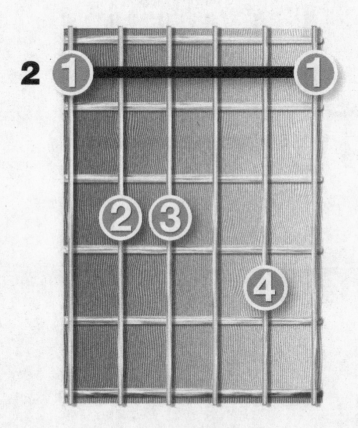

Chord Spelling
1st (F#), ♭3rd (A), 5th (C#), ♭7th (E)

F#/G♭7
Dominant 7th

Chord Spelling
1st (F#), 3rd (A#), 5th (C#), ♭7th (E)

Online access
flametreemusic.com Scan the code
to hear the chord

F#/G♭°7
Diminished 7th

X X

4

① ②

③ ④

Chord Spelling
1st (F#), ♭3rd (A), ♭5th (C), ♭♭7th (E♭)

Online access
flametreemusic.com

Scan the code
to hear the chord

F♯/G♭7sus4
Dominant 7th Suspended 4th

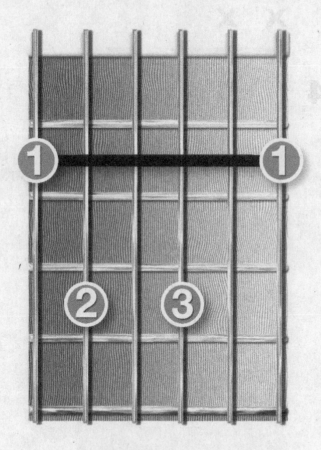

Chord Spelling
1st (F♯), 4th (B), 5th (C♯), ♭7th (E)

F♯/G♭maj9
Major 9th

Chord Spelling
1st (F♯), 3rd (A♯), 5th (C♯), 7th (E♯), 9th (G♯)

F#/G♭m9
Minor 9th

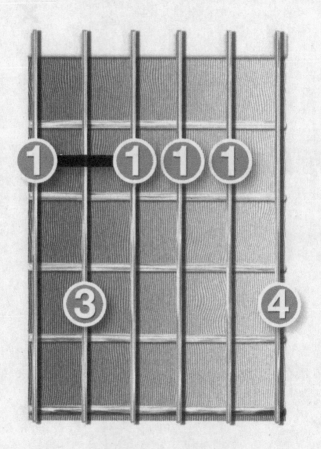

Chord Spelling
1st (F#), ♭3rd (A), 5th (C#), ♭7th (E), 9th (G#)

F♯/G♭9
Dominant 9th

Chord Spelling
1st (F♯), 3rd (A♯), 5th (C♯), ♭7th (E), 9th (G♯)

F#/G♭maj11
Major 11th

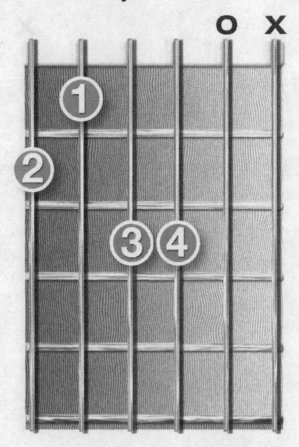

Chord Spelling
1st (F#), 3rd (A#), 5th (C#), 7th (E#), 9th (G#), 11th (B)

Online access
flametreemusic.com

Scan the code
to hear the chord

F♯/G♭maj13
Major 13th

Chord Spelling
1st (F♯), 3rd (A♯), 5th (C♯), 7th (E♯), 9th (G♯), 11th (B), 13th (D♯)

Online access
flametreemusic.com

Scan the code
to hear the chord

G
Major

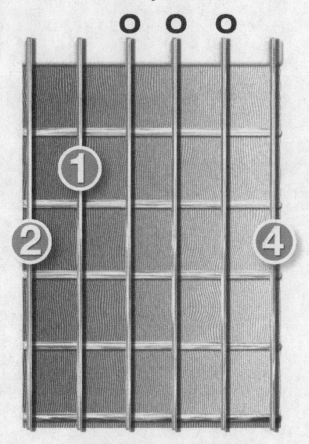

Chord Spelling
1st (G), 3rd (B), 5th (D)

Gm
Minor

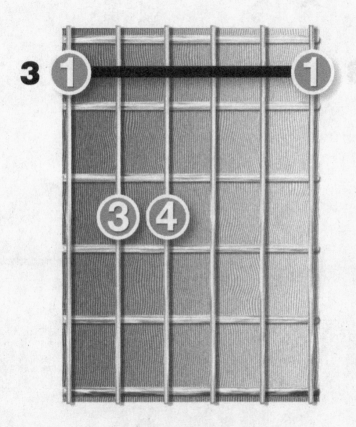

Chord Spelling
1st (G), ♭3rd (B♭), 5th (D)

G+
Augmented Triad

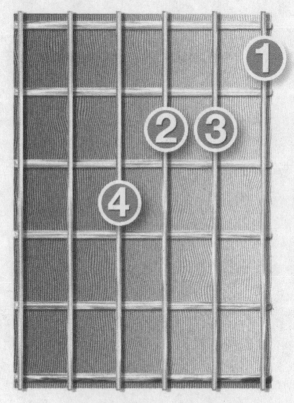

Chord Spelling
1st (G), 3rd (B), ♯5th (D♯)

G°
Diminished Triad

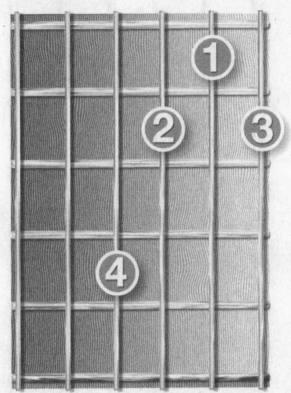

Chord Spelling
1st (G), ♭3rd (B♭), ♭5th (D♭)

Gsus2
Suspended 2nd

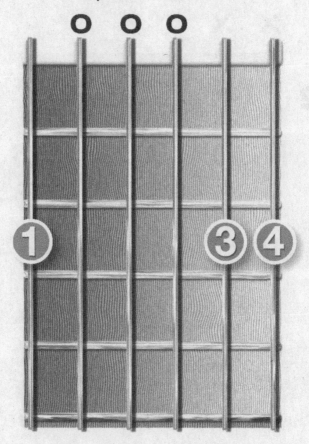

Chord Spelling
1st (G), 2nd (A), 5th (D)

Online access
flametreemusic.com

Scan the code
to hear the chord

Gsus4
Suspended 4th

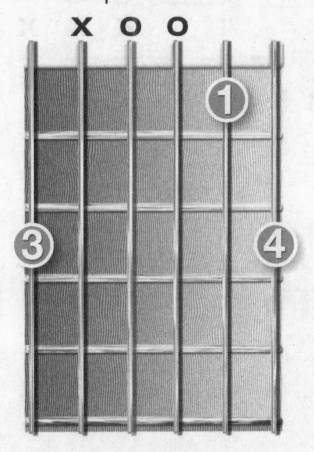

Chord Spelling
1st (G), 4th (C), 5th (D)

G5
5th (Power Chord)

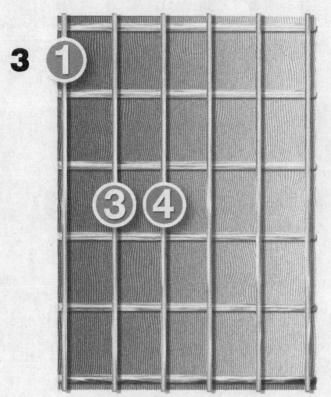

Chord Spelling
1st (G), 5th (D)

G6
Major 6th

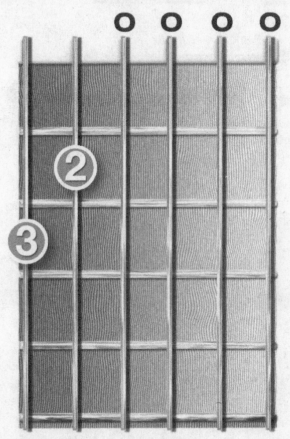

Chord Spelling
1st (G), 3rd (B), 5th (D), 6th (E)

Online access
flametreemusic.com Scan the code
to hear the chord

Gm6
Minor 6th

3

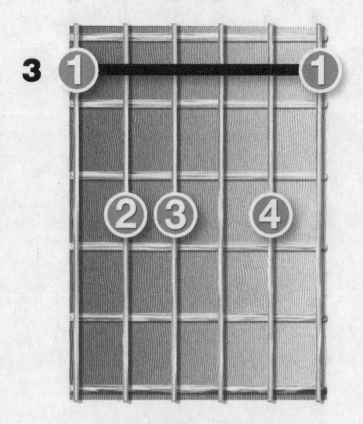

Chord Spelling
1st (G), ♭3rd (B♭), 5th (D), 6th (E)

G6sus4
6th Suspended 4th

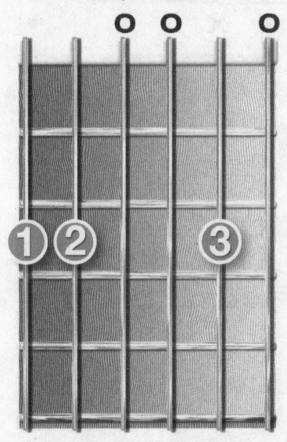

Chord Spelling
1st (G), 4th (C), 5th (D), 6th (E)

Gmaj7
Major 7th

x x

2

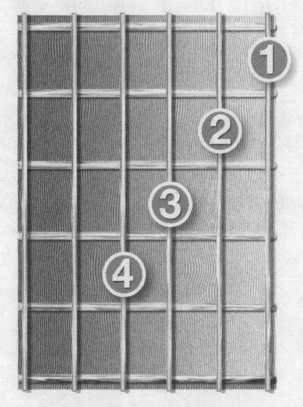

Chord Spelling

1st (G), 3rd (B), 5th (D), 7th (F♯)

Gm7
Minor 7th

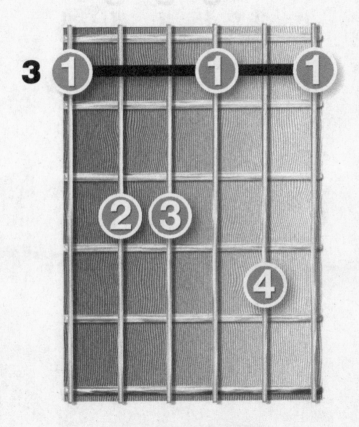

3

Chord Spelling

1st (G), ♭3rd (B♭), 5th (D), ♭7th (F)

G

G7
Dominant 7th

Chord Spelling
1st (G), 3rd (B), 5th (D), ♭7th (F)

Online access
flametreemusic.com Scan the code
to hear the chord

G°7
Diminished 7th

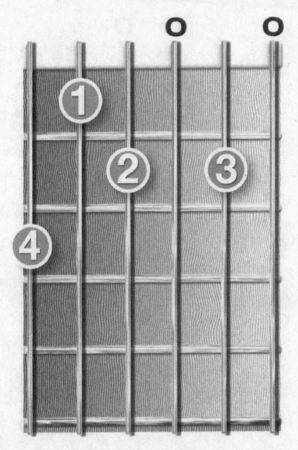

Chord Spelling
1st (G), ♭3rd (B♭), ♭5th (D♭), ♭♭7th (F♭)

G7sus4

Dominant 7th Suspended 4th

Chord Spelling

1st (G), 4th (C), 5th (D), ♭7th (F)

Gmaj9
Major 9th

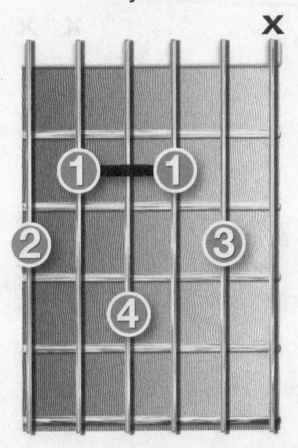

Chord Spelling
1st (G), 3rd (B), 5th (D), 7th (F#), 9th (A)

Gm9
Minor 9th

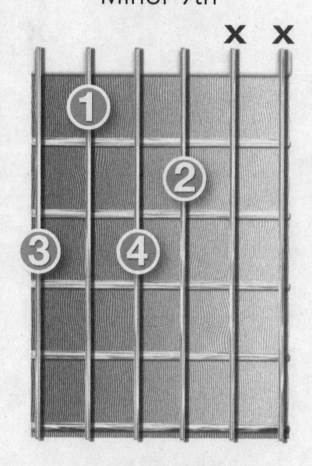

Chord Spelling

1st (G), ♭3rd (B♭), 5th (D), ♭7th (F), 9th (A)

G9
Dominant 9th

Chord Spelling
1st (G), 3rd (B), 5th (D), ♭7th (F), 9th (A)

Gmaj11
Major 11th

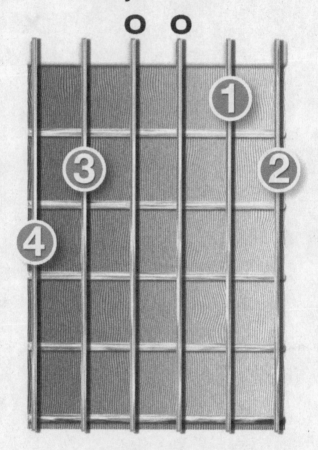

Chord Spelling
1st (G), 3rd (B), 5th (D), 7th (F♯), 9th (A), 11th (C)

Gmaj13
Major 13th

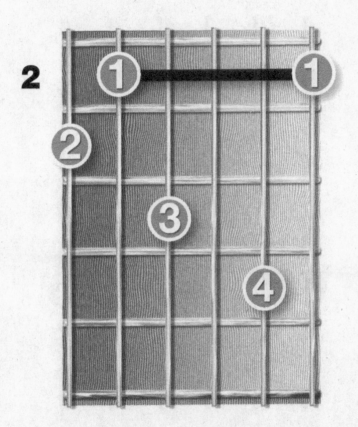

2

Chord Spelling
1st (G), 3rd (B), 5th (D), 7th (F#), 9th (A), 11th (C), 13th (E)

G#/A♭
Major

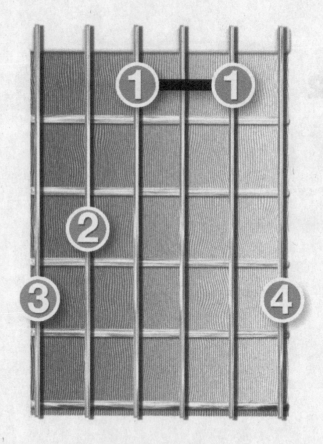

Chord Spelling
1st (A♭), 3rd (C), 5th (E♭)

G#/Abm
Minor

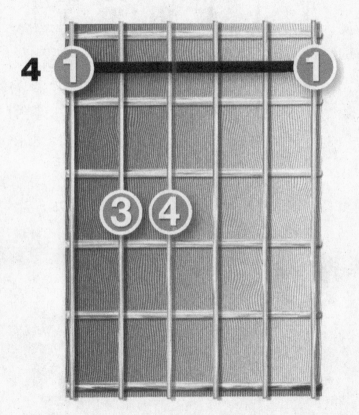

4

Chord Spelling
1st (Ab), b3rd (Cb), 5th (Eb)

G#/A♭+
Augmented Triad

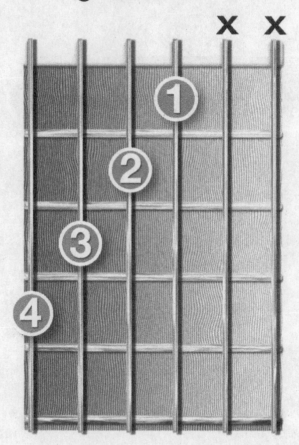

Chord Spelling
1st (A♭), 3rd (C), #5th (E)

G♯/A♭°
Diminished Triad

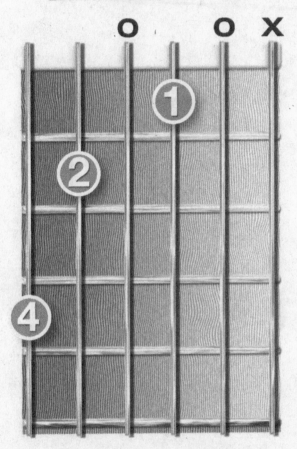

Chord Spelling
1st (A♭), ♭3rd (C♭), ♭5th (E♭♭)

G#/A♭sus2
Suspended 2nd

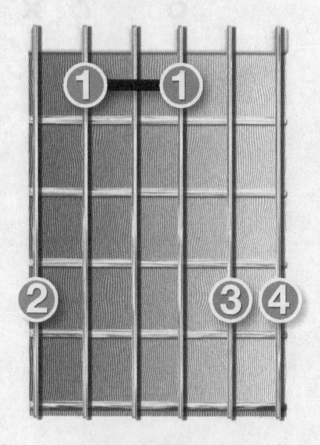

Chord Spelling

1st (A♭), 2nd (B♭), 5th (E♭)

G♯/A♭sus4
Suspended 4th

Chord Spelling
1st (A♭), 4th (D♭), 5th (E♭)

G♯/A♭5
5th (Power Chord)

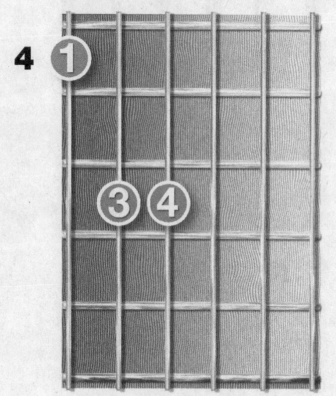

Chord Spelling
1st (A♭), 5th (E♭)

G#/A♭6
Major 6th

Chord Spelling
1st (A♭), 3rd (C), 5th (E♭), 6th (F)

Online access
flametreemusic.com

Scan the code
to hear the chord

G♯/A♭m6
Minor 6th

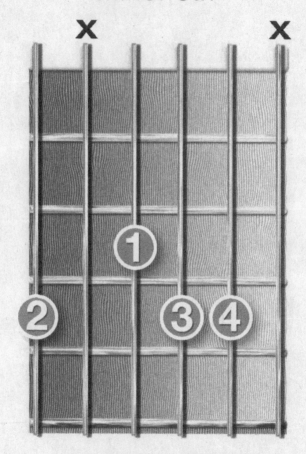

Chord Spelling
1st (A♭), ♭3rd (C♭), 5th (E♭), 6th (F)

G#/A♭6sus4
6th Suspended 4th

Chord Spelling
1st (A♭), 4th (D♭), 5th (E♭), 6th (F)

G♯/A♭maj7
Major 7th

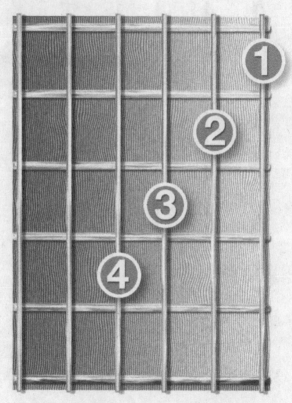

Chord Spelling

1st (A♭), 3rd (C), 5th (E♭), 7th (G)

G♯/A♭m7
Minor 7th

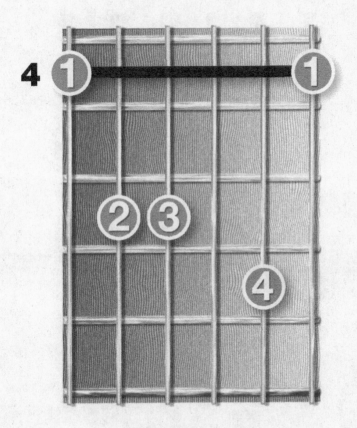

4

Chord Spelling
1st (A♭), ♭3rd (C♭), 5th (E♭), ♭7th (G♭)

G♯/A♭7
Dominant 7th

Chord Spelling

1st (A♭), 3rd (C), 5th (E♭), ♭7th (G♭)

G♯/A♭°7
Diminished 7th

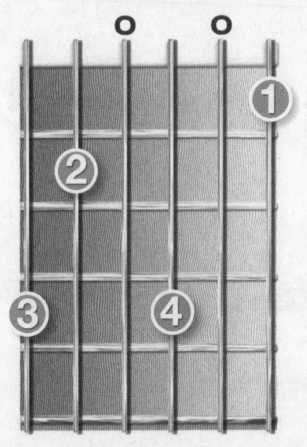

Chord Spelling
1st (A♭), ♭3rd (C♭), ♭5th (E♭♭), ♭♭7th (G♭♭)

G♯/A♭7sus4
Dominant 7th Suspended 4th

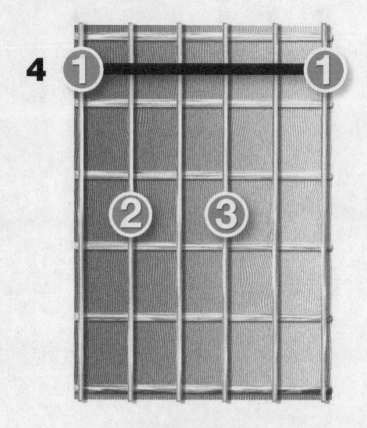

4

Chord Spelling
1st (A♭), 4th (D♭), 5th (E♭), ♭7th (G♭)

G♯/A♭maj9
Major 9th

X

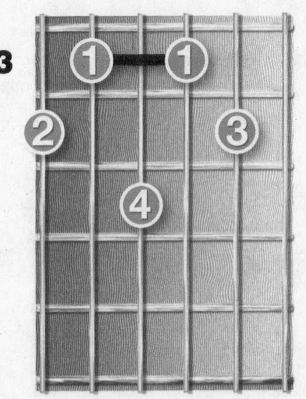

3

Chord Spelling
1st (A♭), 3rd (C), 5th (E♭), 7th (G), 9th (B♭)

G♯/A♭m9
Minor 9th

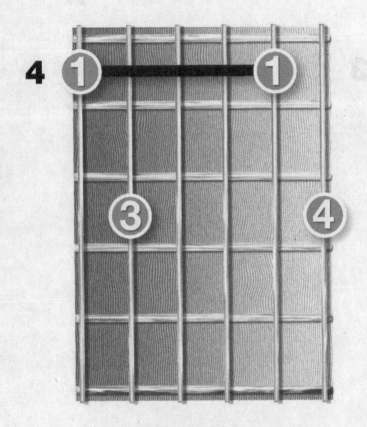

Chord Spelling

1st (A♭), ♭3rd (C♭), 5th (E♭), ♭7th (G♭), 9th (B♭)

G#/A♭9
Dominant 9th

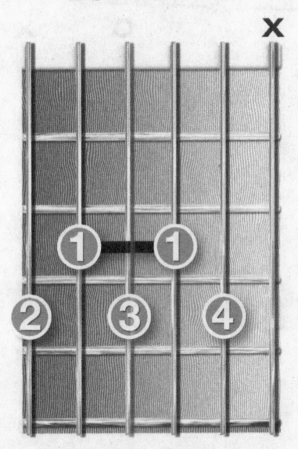

Chord Spelling
1st (A♭), 3rd (C), 5th (E♭), ♭7th (G♭), 9th (B♭)

G♯/A♭maj11
Major 11th

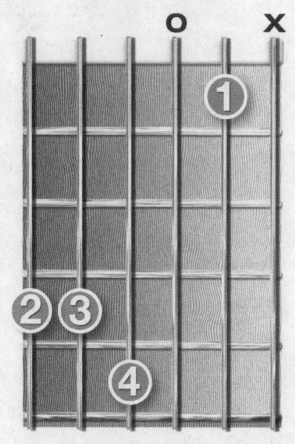

Chord Spelling
1st (A♭), 3rd (C), 5th (E♭), 7th (G), 9th (B♭), 11th (D♭)

G♯/A♭maj13
Major 13th

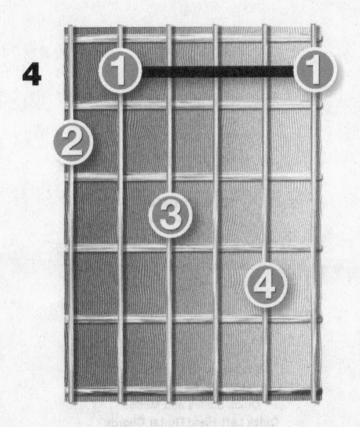

Chord Spelling

1st (A♭), 3rd (C), 5th (B♭), 7th (G), 9th (B♭), 11th (D♭), 13th (F)

Other books in this series:
Quick How to Read Music
Quick Piano & Keyboard Chords
Quick Scales and Modes
Quick Left-Hand Guitar Chords
Quick Ukulele Chords